THE IRISH
ECONOMY
—Past, Present, and Future

THE IRISH ECONOMY
—Past, Present, and Future

CAUSES OF IRISH ECONOMIC RECESSIONS
AND
SOLUTIONS FOR GROWTH

ANDRÉ HAKIZIMANA

iUniverse, Inc.
Bloomington

The Irish Economy—Past, Present, and Future
Causes of Irish Economic Recessions and Solutions for Growth

iUniverse books may be ordered through booksellers or by contacting:

iUniverse
1663 Liberty Drive
Bloomington, IN 47403
www.iuniverse.com
1-800-Authors (1-800-288-4677)

Because of the dynamic nature of the Internet, any web addresses or links contained in this book may have changed since publication and may no longer be valid. The views expressed in this work are solely those of the author and do not necessarily reflect the views of the publisher, and the publisher hereby disclaims any responsibility for them.

Any people depicted in stock imagery provided by Thinkstock are models, and such images are being used for illustrative purposes only.
Certain stock imagery © Thinkstock.

ISBN: 978-1-4759-9174-1 (sc)
ISBN: 978-1-4759-9173-4 (hc)
ISBN: 978-1-4759-9172-7 (ebk)

Library of Congress Control Number: 2013909448

Printed in the United States of America

iUniverse rev. date: 06/20/2013

To Irish economic readers and Irish policymakers

Contents

Preface: Why I Wrote This Book

Psychology literature points out that learning about one's ability does show some bias, in which people overestimate or underestimate the degree to which they are responsible for past successes or failures. According to Hastorf, Schneider, and Polefka (1970, p. 73), "We are prone to credit success to own dispositions and failure to external forces." After the clash of the Anglo-Irish Bank in 2008, some Irish people criticised the government, bankers, and developers for the Irish financial and economic crisis. Others held the international financial crisis and the breakdown of the three largest United States investment banks (Lehman Brothers, Bear Stearns, and Merrill Lynch) as the cause. This context inspired me to carry out research on Irish economic policy before and after Ireland's independence from the United Kingdom. That research turned into this book.

In 2008, I started to search for a way to understand how Irish politicians succeeded or failed in helping their country's economy, but I could not understand that without studying Ireland's economy, Irish markets, and the causes of recessions in those markets, before and after Ireland's independence. This book specifically discusses Ireland's economic issues from an Irish point of view. While this book is about Irish economic strategies, it also addresses facts that caused persistence recessions in the Irish economy. The book clearly identifies what caused the Irish markets to fail in recent years. Some understood the effects of doing nothing and started working together to create healthy growth in the Irish economy.

The ambition of this book is not to criticise Irish policymakers. The goal of this book is to address the origins of Irish economic growth, financial crises, and Irish recessions before and after Ireland's independence from the United Kingdom. In addition, this book shows why Irish economic policies and indigenous enterprises stayed stagnant after independence. In fact, the 2008 recession in Ireland and the current financial crisis in the Irish economy were not caused by either international economic crises or the crash of the Anglo-Irish Bank. The crash of the Anglo-Irish Bank in 2008 was a signal of fundamental problems in the Irish economic strategy. In other words, that crash was not the sole cause of the recession or the current crisis in Irish financial institutions.

First, this book takes readers through literatures that underline Irish society and the development of Irish markets. Part one of this book discusses the Irish economic strategy before independence. It discusses the Irish markets, Irish industry, Irish investments, and Irish innovations. In addition, it addresses the roots of the crisis and recessions in the pre-independence Irish economy. There is no doubt that before its independence from the United Kingdom, the Irish economic growth depended on export to the UK. The Irish exported large quantities of beef and butter to English colonial markets. Thus, the crisis in Irish agriculture was one of the main causes of the country's economic slowdown. On the other hand, banking was the sole cause of Irish economic growth. However, the Irish emigration became a symptom of the lack of job creation in the country.

Part two of this book explains how Irish economic policy developed after the country's independence in 1921.

In general, Irish economic policies have not changed since pre-independence. Its reliance on foreign direct investments (FDI) has a big influence on Irish policymakers, which makes it difficult to create sustainable employment policies. This means that because Irish job creation depends on foreign business investment, there is a negative result when these businesses are no longer interested in bringing more jobs to Ireland.

Despite that, the 2008 Irish recession contributed to crises in Irish housing markets and financial institutions; it originated from closing down of foreign businesses in Ireland. Policymakers were responsible for most Irish economic strategies; this book tries to explore the Irish Public Administration's approach to macroeconomic problems.

Part three of this book examines problems in Irish laws and other policies that drive the Irish economy. I do not believe that the Irish cabinet and departments can help the Irish economy. In 2011, a sum of €3.6 billion figured twice in the Department of Finance report. This was one of many examples of mismanagement in Irish departments. There was also confusion over letters to pensioners about tax liabilities. Finally, this book provides some solutions to grow Irish economy. Sustainable growth requires a radical change in Irish administration; specifically, there must be a total culture change in how departments conduct daily work. There will be no hope to change for good if the Irish economy does not make the needed change.

The weight of all this is a misunderstanding on the effectiveness of Irish policies, which drive its economy and contribute to the country's high unemployment. The origins of sustainable economic growth are neither government spending nor private equity; the answer is in the hands of consumers. In other words, it depends not on government spending or on whether investors want to invest. Economic growth depends on creation of goods and services that people want to consume. Thus, a country's economic growth will come from alternative economic policies that help employment, which in turn raises consumption while increasing investment.

Introduction: The Background to Irish Society

This book examines the origins of Irish economic growth, financial crises, and recessions. Many people believe that any economic growth strengthens and helps society. That is why the book discusses the strengths and weaknesses of Irish society.

In the seventeenth century, the Irish society was unequal. Most of the Irish population were the labouring classes, the cottiers and farm labourers, and they were living in poverty, at the bottom of social hierarchy. These classes continued to expand in the eighteenth and early nineteenth centuries.

The 1841 census divided the Irish population into four categories. The first category included property owners and farmers of more than fifty acres. The second category included artisans and farmers with five to fifty acres. The third category included labourers and smallholders up to five acres. The unspecified fourth category was not numerically significant (Cullen 1972).

For the rural districts of the country, the first two categories accounted for 30 percent of the families. In addition, the rural population of Ireland as a whole consisted of labourers and smallholders, with less than five acres to prosperous artisans. The first two categories combined ranged from as high as 42 percent in some eastern counties to as low as 15 percent in Mayo. The proportion in the first two categories was 30 percent in Monaghan, 30 percent in Cavan, 32 percent in Meat, and 32 percent in Louth. However, the situation had rapidly worsened within the preceding twenty years through the decline of the linen industry.

The proportions of the population in the first two categories ranged from 35 percent in Limerick, 33 percent in Tipperary, and 28 percent in Cork. This region was overall poorer than in the east and in the north of Ireland. The textile industry in this region declined more rapidly than in other parts of the country.

There were low proportions of families falling into the first two categories in counties Donegal, Sligo, Leitrim, Roscommon, Mayo, Galway, and Clare. The proportion did not exceed 23 percent. In all these counties, sharp contrasts existed between better-off and poorer districts. Both Roscommon and Leitrim had concentrations of impoverished smallholders in the north and northwest, and mostly farmers and badly off labourers occupied the south. The same pattern existed within other counties, especially between a poor west and a prosperous east in counties such as Donegal, Sligo, Galway, and Clare. Regions of impoverished smallholders also existed in peninsular Kerry and southwest Cork.

The better-off areas in these counties formed part of the socially and economically intermediate national region centred on the south and midlands. The poorer districts formed an extensive and continual region along the western coast and the hinterland. It was most extensive with County Mayo. In 1841, only 15 percent of the families in Mayo were in the first two census categories. The Poor Law Commission in 1836 reported that Mayo was the most neglected county in Ireland.

In the 1841 census, farms of six to fifteen acres had, on average, two cattle; there were almost as many horses as there were farms in this category. The average value of livestock on holdings of six to fifteen acres was £22.5. On farms of sixteen to thirty acres, the average was £46. Labouring families controlled no livestock, apart from maybe one pig.

The strength of the intermediaries in the eighteenth century was that they had taken their lands on long leases and reset the land on several occasions on short lease rents, which reflected the resulting general upward trend in rents.

Like property owners, intermediaries suffered from rising arrears in the bad years after 1815, given the general rise in rents. Before 1815, they could not hope to renegotiate the renewal of their leases on profitable terms. During the first half of the eighteenth century, the role of intermediaries dwindled, as property owner took more interest in estate management; their numbers rapidly dropped in the decades after 1815. During this period, the property owner's direct relationship with occupants of the estate increased significantly, marking a decline in their direct involvement in economic improvement. Income climbed; it had become more precarious. Spending stayed stable, partly because of rising rent rolls, especially during the Napoleonic period. This kept property owners to a higher standard of living, because of the stability of income from mortgage payments. Thus, property owners decided to decrease investment in properties, to preserve their regular income. There was a huge decrease in the volume of property owner investments in estate management. In addition, there was a significant decrease in local industrial activities and transportation infrastructures. Later in the same century, however, there was a strong show in returning to farming.

The Irish population increased sharply between the middle of the eighteenth century and 1841. Between 1735 and 1785, it rose from 3 million to 4 million. By 1841, it had risen to 8.2 million. The population growth had serious implications, especially for districts where land was scarce and families were pushing out onto barren areas, or for labourers who had to rely on casual employment from farmers and on renting plots. Population growth added the problems of unemployment and poverty. As the population grew and unemployment became more critical, diet worsened. The diet of the poor had become miserable; potatoes and milk became a luxury for many labouring families. Poor families had no savings or assets in case of emergencies. If the potato harvest failed, there was hunger or even starvation. In the poorest regions, cash relief was not a viable solution, since there was no local grocery to buy food. In these regions, occasional potato harvest failures created famines. Here are a couple of these famines: the famine in the southwest in 1822; the Mayo famine in 1831; and the Donegal famine in 1836. Between 1845 and 1851, the Irish population decreased by about two million; this was called "the Great Famine," because it was responsible for such a huge population decline in midcentury. However, some would argue the decline in population was certain, since "the Great Emigration" had begun just before the famine.

Because of the growth in population, and a decline in domestic industry, Ireland was becoming more rural, more agricultural, than it had been. Mayo appeared to be the most industrialised county. Domestic textiles, however, were beginning to experience a crisis. This emerged earliest in wool, and earlier in spinning than weaving. The fact that the woollen industry existed in the southern half of the country explains why occupations outside agriculture in the 1821 census were fewer in Munster than in the other provinces. This was why severe poverty emerged in early data among the labouring classes in Munster at large. The linen industry also declined earlier in

Munster than elsewhere. Bandon, for example, was the centre of the linen industry in the 1780s; the decline in its linen industry affected the decline in wool, and in 1831, the town counted only 375 weavers. According to evidence before the Poor Law Enquiry in 1836, some 4,000 to 5,000 weavers from Cork had gone to the United Kingdom since 1810. Cotton spinning and weaving had been undertaken in many regions, but even before the major crisis of the midtwenties, it was declining in the more peripheral locations. The linen industry stopped expanding after power spinning was introduced in the UK.

While the wealth of Ireland was concentrated in the hands of a few, most people in southern Ireland were living at a subsistence level; their lives depended on the potato crop. So during the Great Famine, between 1845 and 1851, over five million people emigrated in the 1921, most of them young single adults. More than one million Irish people died of starvation, and one and a half million emigrated to North America and the United Kingdom.

The fundamental cause of the Great Famine was not the failure of the potato crop. The origins of the Great Famine was an increase in the price of corn and a lack of capital to increase wages as well as production of corn between 1760 and 1810. As a result, poverty increased due to an unequal distribution of wealth and income in Irish society; the majority of people did not have enough money to buy corn or other food, and consequently, they were the chief victims of the high price of corn.

Because of the fall in agricultural prices after the Great Famine, the landowners extended pasture, leading to a decline in the agricultural labour force. The number of rural labourers fell from 700,000 in 1845 to 300,000 in 1910; the number of cottiers with fewer than five acres also fell, from 300,000 to 62,000. The number of farmers with between five and fifteen acres declined from 310,000 to 154,000. However, the number of farmers with more than fifteen acres rose from 277,000 to 304,000 (Cullen, p. 2).

While pasture became more profitable than grain, the demand for the cottiers and farm labourers declined. Further, agitation for change in the relations between property owners and tenant farmers intensified, resulting in a series of land acts, including the Wyndham Act of 1903. Most tenants bought out their farms with the aid of government loans. However, capital for development was scarce, and investors became less willing to take risks. The instability of farm incomes also led to a reduction in farm development.

Before the 1800s, the Irish Parliament encouraged industry development through tariff subsidies or grants. As many new industries sprang up, prosperity in this decade grew. Textile industries and the domestic industry expanded but then declined after the Act of Union in 1801, which bound Ireland more closely to the United Kingdom. In effect, the act abolished the Irish Parliament. In 1841, a provision was created to remove tariffs between Ireland and the UK. By 1907, the brewing industry in Dublin and shipbuilding in Belfast prospered, but the textile industries were in decline.

In 1921, Ireland became the Irish Free State, comprising thirty-two counties (six counties, known as Northern Ireland, remained part of the United Kingdom); in 1949, the country withdrew from the British Commonwealth and became the Republic of Ireland. Ireland's population was 4,354,000 in 1921; 71 percent lived in the twenty-six counties known as southern Ireland. Ireland joined the European Economic Community (EEC) in 1973.

As the Irish Free State, in the first years of independence, free trade continued with the United Kingdom, and economic policy concentrated chiefly on raising agricultural efficiency. The country's overall prosperity depended on agriculture and on the export market. In this period, food and drink amounted to 85 percent of total goods exported. Further, the United Kingdom provided a huge market for Irish livestock products. In the 1920s, farm incomes were free from income taxation. In 1927, the Irish government decided to cut the standard income tax rate from 25 percent, which had begun in 1924. Income tax receipts amounted to 3 percent of the gross national product, and nearly three-quarters of total revenue came from indirect taxes, mainly customs and excise duties and local authority rates on property.

However, in this period, agriculture faced difficult conditions caused by a drop in prices in 1924. The volume of gross agricultural output in 1924 to 1925 was 13 percent below the level of 1912 to 1913. In addition to the civil war, which affected production, there were poor harvests in 1923 to 1924 because of poor weather. Even though the output had recovered by over 10 percent in 1929 to 1930, it was still 4 percent below the prewar level.

In this decade, the Land Act of 1923 completed the transfer of land from property owners to small peasant owners. In addition, in 1927, the Agricultural Credit Corporation was established to provide loans to farmers.

From to 1926 to 1929, the total volume of industrial output rose 8 percent; however, there was a great slowdown from 1929 to 1931, when the output was less than 2 percent. Because of the lack of progress in employment creation, emigration continued. From 1921 to 1931, emigration increased to average 33,000 a year; the average in 1901 to 1911 was 26,000 a year, and in 1911 to 1921, it was 19,000 a year. The estimated decline in population from 1922 to 1931 was roughly 10 percent a year.

Emigration declined after the United States tightened its immigration laws and job opportunities abroad fell as a result of the Great Depression. For the first time since the Great Famine, in 1931, emigration was less than 9,000; the movement to the United States became insignificant, falling to 256 in 1932. In these circumstances, the total population that had dropped every year since independence rose by 11,000 in 1931 and continued to rise. In this period, the volume of export fell by 10 percent. New jobs needed to be created, but the Irish government was still struggling to create sustainable jobs that would allow the people to be productive in their country. Meenan took the view that

> The aims of economic policy have never been so clearly defined, nor its methods so exactly adapted to those aims, as in the first ten years of the State when priority was given to encourage agriculture and Patrick Hogan directed agricultural policy. (Kieran, Giblin, and McHugh 1988, p. 39)

Although it has been some years of economic growth in Ireland after Ireland independence from the United Kingdom, since independence, the Irish government continues to lag behind in investing in Irish location-based services to sustain the Irish economy. In other words, the government was able to create and develop the Irish-based services as core competences in the world economies. In addition, Ireland continues to face a period of low growth and high unemployment because of its economy dependent on export and on foreign direct investments (FDI). A slowdown in international trade, and thus international economic and foreign direct investments in Ireland, presents challenges for Ireland achieving sustainable economic conditions. Ireland needs investments in the Irish-based services; otherwise, its high unemployment will remain persistently over the next decade.

Part I: Pre-independence Ireland

MARKETS DEVELOPMENT

In the sixteenth and seventeenth centuries, the United Kingdom conquered Ireland's markets. In doing so, the English changed Irish markets and Irish society. They overthrew the island nation's legal rights to its lands, confiscated those lands, and resettled them. The minority English settlers had the power to transform Irish economic activities into those more favourable to their interests. They created an unequal society by introducing a new system based on ethnic class between the native Irish and the English settlers. This system enabled English settlers to seek wealth at the expense of stability for the Irish people. Introducing new farming techniques and reducing Irish peasants to tenants and labourers created enormous wealth. By 1689, the transformation of Irish land was complete. The seventeenth century was a period of transition of Ireland's economy towards the interest of the English trade. Then came new authority in Ireland, and the new rules were sympathetic to English commerce. Ireland was divided into counties with English courts and judges. Brehon, the native Irish law, became illegal. Soldiers and new settlers had the power to collect taxes and enforce new laws.

Besides these powers, town patrons received grants to hold profitable markets (Hunter 1971, pp. 41, 48–49). In addition, towns were in the hands of a small, self-elected group who set up civil courts, imposed fines and punishment, and had the power to send members to the Dublin Parliament.

Corporations gained power over economic and political decisions. They controlled local trade and enforced public laws, such as those on public health and education. In this context, penal laws turned the indigenous population into noncitizens. The acts of 1695 and 1704 forbade Catholics from studying abroad, excluded native Irish from owning property or serving in professions, and created oaths of allegiance for public office (Foster 1988, p. 153). James II threatened to reverse the Protestant monopoly power, but settler resistance led to his overthrow.

According to Barnard (1979, p. 171), Protestant domination of borough governments became one of the most enduring Cromwellian legacies in Ireland. Cromwell barred Catholics from local government and merchant trades. He also physically removed them from the towns.

As a result, Irish Catholic merchants lost control of their small fleet, ending their trade with Europe. For example, Galway merchants had notable trade with Spain, Portugal, France, and West Indies. However, to make Ireland markets more dependent on the English, Cromwell removed the Irish Catholics from towns and cut their contacts with Europe and America. In this way, the capacities and long-term development of the Irish merchant class dwindled. Cromwellian policies centralised political and economic strategies in Dublin. As a result, Dublin became the centre of the trade link between Britain and Ireland. Besides, Irish production became dependent on England. Administration, law, education, and other state roles such as taxation catered around Dublin, which also became a centre of export-import trade. As the Irish continental trade was destroyed, smaller towns, which did not share in Dublin's power, declined. The country's merchant marine also declined, destroying Ireland's merchant class.

Even though Dublin became the centre of export-import trade, by the 1730s, Cork was the centre for Irish exports. During 1772–1800, more than half of Irish beef exports came from Cork, while the rest came from nearby Waterford (O'Donovan 1940, p. 117). Agnew (1994) wrote that the provisions trade was also an important source of developing the merchant community in Belfast, which would later become the north's industrial capital.

During the sixteenth and seventeenth centuries, the English changed Ireland's markets structure through confiscation and settlement. While transforming Irish markets, they established systems that served their own interests. According to Crotty (1966, p. 6), English soldiers and new settlers came to Ireland as apostles of the new order of individualism, with little regard for the security of the masses.

During the seventeenth century, the United Kingdom had the power to control transatlantic markets by direct military force and through regulatory infrastructures, such as creating the Navigation Acts, which gave English merchants the right to drive transatlantic markets and limited Irish markets. Under the Staple Act of 1693, only servants, horses, and food were shipped directly from Ireland to the colonies.

The act also placed a prohibitively high duty on Irish cattle exports to the United Kingdom. According to O'Donovan, Irish cattle exports went mainly to the Atlantic maritime trade. Exportation increased in 1665 at 33 percent, changing to 96 percent by 1669. Nevertheless, the 1665 Cattle Bill restricted exports of Irish cattle, sheep, and supplies. The bill needed renewal every year until it became permanent in 1680. As a result, the Cattle Bills affected the Irish standard of living. After 1665, total cattle exports fell by half and did not reach 1665 levels again until 1716.

In addition, Irish wool exports were banned outside the UK. The bills also produced a powerful civil society in the United Kingdom. Therefore, dominant classes exercised political power through Parliament. The royal policy was to encourage and tax Irish cattle exports.

After 1770, the United Kingdom embargoed Irish supplies and linen exports to France and the American colonies. After 1776, because of the American War of Independence, Irish supplies were exported only to the United Kingdom, which then re-exported them to the colonies. However, in 1778, there was an embargo on Irish exports to the United Kingdom. The effects of these embargoes were severe. Barrelled beef exports fell by 40 percent between 1772 and 1792 and never recovered. Exports to France, which made up a third of beef exports in 1764, fell nearly to zero in 1780 (O'Donovan 1940, p. 125). Ireland's position rebounded after the removal of embargoes on exports to the United Kingdom. Opening the English food markets increased Irish butter, ham, and bacon exports, while barrelled beef exports continued to decline. Irish supplies consistently undersold English supplies because of cheap Irish labour (O'Donnell 1940, p. 66; Edie 1940, p. 41).

In 1778, the acts that excluded direct trade with Ireland changed, but the Irish still could not directly export to the colonies (Harper 1939, pp. 401–2). The original goals of trade limits were not only to suppress Ireland's economy but also to encourage the production of commodities and services that were important to the United Kingdom's trade.

By 1800, the UK became the main market for Irish beef and pork because of the high demand in British colonial territories.

INDUSTRY

Irish industries needed support to develop markets in Ireland. In addition, investors of Irish capital had to compete with low-cost labour instead of innovating. They had few options to choose from, which was major blowback. For example, clustered innovating sectors like engineering and textile finishing were all concentrated in the United Kingdom.

So not only was Irish industry less mechanised than the United Kingdom's, it also relied on the UK for its machinery, as well as everyday supplies, from rollers and spindles to mill gearing. Thus, while Ireland had freer access to UK machinery, it had become dependent on British engineering. In addition, Ireland's dependence on English channels of supply was the result of its weak position in the global economy. This prevented Ireland from settling the market connections and naval capacities that would enable access to raw materials from world markets.

In 1614, limits on Irish wool exports were tightened. In 1615, only licensed exporters were authorised to export to the United Kingdom. In addition, very few Irish ports were licensed to export wool to the UK in 1617. This measure stopped Ireland from supplying the United Kingdom's continental competitors (O'Donovan 1940, p. 41). In 1619, the law allowed exports only with a special warrant, but the Irish continuously complained that not enough warrants were available. After 1632, the Lord Deputy of Ireland granted export licenses more freely, because discouraging wool exports actually encouraged the Irish to develop home-grown woollen manufacturing (O'Donovan 1940, pp. 42–43). Finally, a request to export wool, skins, and yarn to the United Kingdom was approved in 1641. The English encouraged Irish home spinning of yarn for the British weaving industry.

However, in 1660, English policy discouraged the emerging Irish woollen industries by high import duties. The high duties stopped Irish woollens from entering the English markets. In 1662, Charles II directed the lord lieutenant to grant licenses freely for wool exports for fear that Ireland would otherwise make up its own woollen fabrics and compete with United Kingdom manufacturing. Ireland's lower labour costs gave it competitive advantages over the English manufacturers. At this stage, in the 1670s, the Irish Parliament passed protectionist duties to help local manufacturers increase their share of the Irish markets. By 1680, Irish woollens were competing on English markets. Exports of Irish frieze rose from 279,722 yards in 1641 to 444,381 in 1665, and 753,189 in 1683 to 1,129,716 in 1687 (Murray 1903, p. 104; Cullen 1972, p. 23). Ireland's textile industry began in woollens and expanded rapidly after 1670. In addition, not only did Irish woollen goods compete on English markets, they also used up raw wool that English industries needed. In 1676, London merchants petitioned the crown to stifle the infant Irish industry. Edie (1970, p. 51) points out the common political sentiment in the United Kingdom was to crush competitive Irish trades and make Ireland a supplier of raw material and a consumer of English goods. Profits from woollens increased property owners' incomes beyond what they could obtain from rents.

Bristol economist John Cary's influential 1695 *Pamphlet Essay on Trade* proposed restricting imports of Irish woollens (Kelly 1980). The first attempt in the English Parliament to prevent Irish woollen exports failed to pass in 1697. There was substantial support for the embargo, but members of Parliament disagreed about whether to restrict exports or ban them outright; they also disagreed about what to do with Irish producers who were forced out. In 1696, the English Board of Trade was set up to find a way to acquire linen from within the empire to relieve English dependence on Baltic linen (Kelly 1980).

Linen was profitable only in areas with low labour costs; core English producers neglected their manufacturers. Therefore, that division into linen was the surest way of breaking the Irish woollen industry. The English Parliament removed import duties on Irish linens. In this period, John Locke inquired in Dublin about Irish manufacturers of linen on behalf of the Board of Trade (Kearney 1959). Locke proposed a scheme for the gradual discouragement of Irish woollen manufacturers by increasing import duties on wool, subsidising the planting of flax, obligating everyone not on the poor rate to produce a stated quantity of flax and yarn, and setting up working schools and competitions to increase weaving and spinning skills.

The board reported to the king, reaffirming its support for reserving the woollen industry for the United Kingdom by transforming Irish production to the manufacture of linen (Kelly 1980). Thus, the preferred route of action was for the Irish themselves to dismantle their woollen trade. Additionally, the secretary of state for Ireland in the English Privy Council had a bill drawn up for the Irish Parliament, which aimed to divert Irish production from wool to linen (Kearney 1959, p. 488). However, the Irish Parliament did not pass the bill, in part because the manufacturers were English settlers. Furthermore, the Irish linen industry was concentrated among Scottish Presbyterians in Ulster (Kearney 1959). In that way, the divergent English Protestants and Scots Presbyterians turned the Irish Parliament against encouraging linen at the expense of the woollen industry.

Finally, the English Parliament passed the Woollen Act in 1699, prohibiting Irish woollen exports. The Woollen Act directly forbade exports of Irish cloth to the United Kingdom and its colonial markets. As result, the Irish woollen industry failed to expand. The UK encouraged Irish linen, as it discouraged woollens after the 1690s. Violations of the Woollen Act carried fines, which also encouraged Irish linen production. In 1696, plain Irish linen was allowed to enter the UK duty free and a linen board was established in 1711. In 1700, the UK funded a colony of Huguenot weavers in a scheme to boost linen production around Belfast. Other skilled immigrants with capital and experience in producing broadcloth textiles looked at Ireland (Gill 1925; Cohen 1990).

The Irish linen sector grew rapidly during the eighteenth century and was the source of Ireland's economic development. In the mid-eighteenth century, linen surpassed livestock and provisions in value, and by the end of the century, linen exports were more than twice as valuable as livestock and provisions. Nevertheless, the linen industry was dependent on the English market. During the eighteenth century, the English market bought more than 90 percent of Irish exports. Increases in linen output in the eighteenth century were the result of using more labour rather than mechanisation or organisational innovation. Most Irish weavers were male farmers and cottiers who wove during the winter months and outside of farming hours. Their raw material supply and markets limited the development of linen and provisions. Linen faced long-term problems of raw material supply, because of limitations to domestic flax cultivation. Moreover, after the suppression of the Irish native merchant class in the seventeenth century, Irish merchants still tried to reach continental markets in linen and other products. However, English maritime policy and the Navigation Acts gave UK traders competitive advantages that the Irish could not overcome.

For the next two hundred years, the Irish markets faced largely disadvantageous competition from other textiles, most noticeably cotton. High value-added stages of production such as printing and dyeing remained in the United Kingdom. Further, linen offered fewer linkages to sectors like machine building and transport. The Irish industries depended on English inputs, technologies, transport, distribution, and finance. Certain geographic regions faced linen scarcity, with Ulster the largest producer. Limited in its ability to induce the rates of technology, and particularly limited in its ability to act as linkages to other regional economic activities, the industry had to rely on outside investors to improve its capacity to do well.

On the contrary, Irish linen entrepreneurs could not compete by introducing technology or factory organisation. Their advantage was in cheap domestic labour.

The predominant organisational characteristic of linen was the long survival of its domestic system of production. Throughout the countryside, there were spreads of farmers who also spun or wove. Irish linen predominated until 1820, and hand weaving played a central role in Irish linen in the 1870s.

As linen stagnated during 1770–1780, the semi-independent Irish Parliament encouraged cotton manufacturers. New spinning technologies were introduced, including water-driven mills. Cotton progressively replaced linen in northeastern Ireland. Monaghan (1942, p. 3) reports that in 1760, there were 400 linen and cotton looms in the Belfast region, while the 1810 census reported 860 cotton looms and six linen looms. Merchants and property owners also attempted, with varying degrees of success, to set up cotton manufacturing elsewhere in Ireland. Irish cotton production expanded rapidly before 1800. A closer look shows that the Irish cotton industry went through two stages. Cotton output grew rapidly and smoothly until the mid-1790s, and then it became slower and more erratic. Before 1801, Irish cotton output grew at 7 percent, but then the growth rate fell dramatically, to 2.6 percent. Besides, Irish cotton output was much less stable after 1802; Irish cotton output was more unstable, with periods of high output and equally distinctive declines.

In 1816, the Irish cotton industry finally collapsed after the UK removed Irish tariffs on yarn (cloth tariffs were removed in 1824). Between 1825 and 1835, Irish yarn output fell from 3.6 million pounds to 2.3 million pounds (Irish Railway Commissions 1837). At this phase, the Manchester manufacturers began to export finished cloth to Ireland. Before 1815, the English cloth exports to Ireland averaged less than 80,000 yards, but they reached 850,000 yards in 1822.

The industry's recovery in the 1820s coincided with the spread of power spinning in Ireland. Its introduction marked the end of domestic linen spinning, which contracted rapidly in traditional districts in the 1830s; yarn spun by homemakers virtually ended in 1841. As factory spinning concentrated in the northeast, weaving came with it. The decay of the cotton industry led thousands of specialist weavers in the neighbourhood of Belfast to move back into linen. The farmer-weavers, faced with a decline in the local output of yarn as well as with completing specialist weavers in the hinterland of Belfast, found themselves unable to compete.

The industry declined rapidly in Monaghan, Fermanagh, Cavan, Louth, and Longford counties and in north Meath, which had long-established traditions in linen.

Drogheda in 1831 still employed 941 males above twenty years in the textile industry. Drogheda in fact had fared better than most areas, because it could replace some of the declining domestic employment by factory textile work.

In the 1841 census, one in five of the population worked in textiles. Textiles gained a reputation of keeping jobs, especially for women. It was a major income provider for rural populations.

The decline in textiles explains the weakening social conditions in many smallholding districts in the pre-famine periods. Except Dublin and Belfast, many medium and smaller centres stagnated in population, and some declined (for example, marine centres such as Kinsale and Cobh). Estate villages, estate towns, and textile centres outside the north also stagnated.

Even though Irish industries were lacking, Northern Ireland had a much stronger linen export industry in the eighteenth century. In the early nineteenth century, the value of linen exports from Ireland, particular from Belfast, exceeded exports of cattle and corn. The cotton industry started in 1777, expanded considerably in the next forty years for home markets, and enjoyed protection from the Irish Parliament. The removal of protection from cotton in 1824 threatened the future of textile production in Belfast, but this was offset by technological development in linen. The technology for the power spinning of flax improved greatly in 1825, ensuring concentration of spinning in Northern Ireland. Belfast was more export-oriented than Dublin.

The mechanisation of linen weaving started in the 1850s. This was the result of a strong competitive position; Belfast linen rapidly captured markets from British linen centres. The next major industry to develop in Belfast was shipbuilding; it ensured the continued industrial development of Belfast until the end of the American Civil War in 1865. Lee concluded that Belfast's progress after 1848 was increasingly due to "immigrant businessmen" (1973, p. 16). Immigrant businessmen liked Belfast, and flourished there, because of the more favourable industrial milieu. Whatever initial advantages the Belfast area possessed in the way of a more settled agricultural system, a more extensive domestic textile industry, and a key trading centre, became bigger over time as industrial skills sharpened, venture capital increased, and success in one activity opened up other possibilities.

INNOVATION AND COMMUNICATION

During 1780–1820, cotton-spinning innovations helped Ireland to compete in a global economy. The mechanisation of machine building, shipping, and distribution played a big role during this period. However, Irish weaving did not move out from people's homes. The industry stayed in small weaving sheds. The only way to get out from that rudimentary industry was to expand, by adding more labour. Nevertheless, spinners competed by intensifying labour exploitation and accepting lower profits rates; weavers in general adapted to the increased supply of yarn by labour-intensive processes. To combat technical disadvantages in spinning, Irish entrepreneurs used labour-intensive methods to compete with English weavers.

Despite low wages for weavers, Irish cloth markets were unstable. In addition, spinning was the first textile sector to feel the effects of recession (Ellison 1886, pp. 78–79). Ireland's market links were weak, and its cotton industry become dependent on the UK markets. Persisting land looms was a rational response to the low price of Irish linen (Geary 1989, p. 263).

The Irish failure to innovate in cotton spinning was a rational response to a market saturated with imports. The more unstable the supply of yarn was, the more precarious the Irish weaving markets were, lacking as they were in capital. Without innovation, Irish weaving was in an unpromising position, falling significantly between the 1820s and the 1850s (Gill 1925, p. 327). The use of power looms in the United Kingdom drove down the handloom weavers throughout Ireland. In the end, many Irish weavers lost their jobs after the fall of the Irish industry.

With a rapid increase in communication, some Irish towns expanded their economic activity into regions with higher population growth. However, the increase in communication dominated the well-situated towns, which waxed rich at the expense of less well-situated neighbours. Youghal, Middleton, Mallow, Kanturk, and Tralee grew, while Dingle, Cobh, and Kinsale became port towns. Doneraile or Lismore changed to estate towns, but industrial centres such as Bandon declined or stagnated. In the midlands, Tullamore, Maryboro, and Mountmellick expanded, while Mountrath, Porttrarlington, Kilbeggan, and Philipstown declined. Navan grew while Trim, Kells, and Athboy stagnated. In Galway, Gort, Tuam, and Ballinasloe market centres grew while Castlebar centre and Westport port stagnated.

The contractions of the Grand Canal to the Shannon and Blanches to Ballinasloe ended in 1804, and the Royal Canal was started in 1817. It took seventeen years to open Mountmellick and Kilbeggan canal. From 1800, a Board of Directors of Inland Navigation was charged with promoting works on navigations; it was transferred to the Boards of Works after 1831. The Shannon navigation dominated the first half of the century, until the completion of Ulster Canal between the Blackwater and the Erne between 1825 and 1842. Ballinamore and Ballyconnell Canal from the Erne to the Shannon took almost twenty years to complete; it started its operations in 1860. That was the steamship era, which helped to revolutionise transport on the Shannon.

Road building advanced rapidly in the early nineteenth century. There were road contractions in the more remote areas such as Connemara and much of west Mayo. Since 1832, parliamentary grants were available to help road contractions. This was the effectiveness of the Board of Works, created in 1831 to take over the management or supervision of the state's interest in roads.

Kilrush was originally was a poor and remote property owner and fishing town, with bad communication. However, steam navigation on the Shannon estuary, opening up the hinterland, behind road building between 1822 and 1841 revolutionised the town. It emerged as an active commercial town. Communication was vital to the economic changes taking place in the early nineteenth century. Towns and merchants who gained from improved communication were eager to see more improvements. The railway system, as it began to take shape from the 1830s, was a response to economic changes as much as a cause of change. Cheapened transport completely shaped the industrial organisation. Certain towns expanded their commerce at the expense of other towns.

Improved communication led to changes in industrial and commercial organisations, when industrial reorganisation took place. The reorganisation entailed the transition of industry from domestic to factory buildings. Although activity had always organised in a factory-type building and often in towns, even village re-organisation was extensive. Many of the country brewers were mere artisan firms; by 1837, they had all become factory units. In 1790, producing beer was around 45 percent in Dublin. It took almost a half century to change to 30 percent, in 1837. Similarly, the distilling industry became highly competitive all over Ireland. The three major distilling centres, Dublin, Cork, and Belfast, accounted for 40 percent of national output in 1836.

During this period, the volume of commercial transactions rose and influenced the growth of banking. A 1782 statute created the Bank of Ireland to increase the banking facilities in the country. It held the government accountable. In addition, merchants and other banks often rediscounted with it the bills of exchange they received from their own customers.

Its notes grew more rapidly, because of the rapid rise in government spending and borrowing during the Napoleonic wars.

Economic Growth, Crisis, and Recessions

Pointed out in the first pages of this book, the most important feature in the growth of Irish trade was the English market that imported cattle, sheep, beef, wool, and some dairy products like butter. A bill containing many prohibitions such as duty on cattle or sheep imported from Ireland came into effect in 1664. Meanwhile, another bill proposal that asked the total exclusion of Irish cattle and sheep easily passed in the Commons in 1665. The following year, they passed another bill that excluded Irish beef and pork. As a result, between 1664 and 1667, the Irish economy declined. This showed that Irish economic growth was dependent on foreign markets. Ireland's capacity to export its commodities in turn was dependent both on the conditions and on growth of foreign markets. For example, in 1683, France imported 43 percent of total Irish exports, but in 1685, when it improved its self-sufficiency, Irish butter was subject to a fairly stiff duty. Irish beef imported into France incurred a prohibitive import in 1688; suddenly, Irish export prices fell to their lowest. Thus, at the end of the 1680s, low prices were evidence of the decrease in Irish economic growth.

Despite French trade restrictions, Irish grain was imported during the French famines of 1693–1694 and 1696. Ireland had good harvests and plenty of corn. The shortages of grain in Europe helped to ensure the Irish grain export at high prices. Good harvests and high prices together spelled prosperity for the Irishman. It increased the real income of many ordinary people. A contemporary writing from Dublin in September 1699 wrote:

> The great failure of corn in Europe for a year or two past, which gave the countery an opportunity of raising theire corne to a very high price, which because we could not import any from abroad, we were not able to bring down ye rates which were not rais'd through any scarcity at home;

> this has enriched ye plowman who always heretofore sold his
> corne to pay his rent . . . this sort of people are in a better
> condition than ever I know them to be. They are generally ye
> native Irish for its rare to heare of an Englishman ever able to
> pay his rent by ye plow. (Cullen 1972, p. 28)

In the 1720s, the Irish economy was on its way to a slowdown.
Despite the good harvests in the early 1720s, there were also
good harvests in Europe. Consequently, agricultural exports
fell in volume. Additionally, there was no growth in this period
because of three successive bad harvests in 1728.

The 1730s marked the beginning of a long period of rapid
growth in Irish exports. Because of the growth in linen, the
volume of linen exports grew rapidly in every subsequent
period. In this decade, exports rose from £1,043,050 in 1730 to
£1,259,853 in 1740.

In the 1780s, grain began to re-emerge as a significant export.
Grains and butter soared both in volume and in price during
the period of the Napoleonic wars. Finally, Irish butter exports
to France declined, starting in the 1730s. The rise in exports
was remarkable because of the continued growth in linen and
grain. Between 1793 and 1815 there were periods of boom. The
volume of exports rose by 40 percent. Nevertheless, despite the
rise of volume exports, the standard of living rose, due more
to the rise in prices than in volume. Exports, valued at current
prices, rose by 120 percent.

The Irish growth in exports was mainly with the transatlantic
traffic and with the United Kingdom. The Irish largely exported
beef and butter to the English colonial market. The supply
of cattle had contracted after the Cattle Acts, and beef prices
had fallen to a lower level, but they were remarkably stable by
comparison with butter prices. The main source of demand
for beef came from the slave populations of West Indian

plantations. Between the 1760s and 1770s, more Irish exports went to English colonies and France.

The grain harvest was hugely important in the Irish economic growth and standard of good living. A bad harvest meant a scarcity of food and rising food prices. Thus if a harvest was superabundant, this resulted in a fall in food prices. A good harvest did not always make the farmer happy. However, the benefit of lower prices raised the real incomes of townspeople and rural labourers and artisans, and rising real incomes stimulated industry. Good harvests meant that exports of grain increased. In contrast, bad harvests increased imports.

Variations in economic activities, from one season to another, were also a function of the harvest. Roughly half the harvests were likely to be average or above, and the other half were below average. So there was a certain regularity about the variations in economic activity; a good harvest then translated into growth, rising revenue, and higher output of industrial goods. A bad harvest, on the other hand, depressed economic activity, revenue, and industrial output, often for a year or two. Within each decade of the century, there were one or two years of growth and one or two years of economic slowdown. The remaining years changed to an intermediate degree of prosperity or depression. It became obvious that when harvests were bad, Irish economic recessions always followed. During the depression, an important outcome, usually after a bad harvest, was the rise in imports. Because imports rose relative to exports, bills of exchange financed by earnings overseas were rare, which made the rate of exchange responsible for the rise in interest for all bills of exchange. Faced with these difficulties, many merchants went bankrupt. Many of their customers were insolvent, and the banks often became suspect as well. As a result, bankers experienced a run by the holders of their notes, eager to exchange them for cash.

In general, pre-independence, the crisis in agriculture was the main cause of the Irish economic slowdown. The agricultural crisis of 1820 in the south of Ireland was largely the effect of an already weak market in the United Kingdom. Potato failures in 1817 and 1819 had already brought suffering, and there was widespread famine affecting the poor in the south in 1882. Low commodity prices had lessened the living standards of the farming community.

All agricultural prices fell sharply after 1815, the prices of grain being low around 1820. However, grain prices recovered in the second half of the 1820s, and again after falling sharply at the end of the 1820s, they rose again in the second half of the 1830s. Prices of livestock products also recovered well in the second half of the 1830s. Despite the decline in beef and pork exports, the volume of agricultural exports rose in the 1820s and 1830s. Exports of livestock doubled between the 1820s and 1830s and doubled again by the mid-1840s. Butter exports in 1824–1827 were 40 percent above exports in 1808–1810. The most remarkable expansion was in exports of grain and flour. From less than a million quarters a year in the first eighteen years of the century, they doubled in the 1820s and climbed to above three million quarters in 1837 and 1838.

With the well off, there was little famine in the eastern counties or in the north. In the midlands and the south, the effects of famine dominated the labouring population, as opposed to the rural community. It was only in the poor regions of the west that failure of the potato presented whole regions with the threat of starvation.

INVESTMENTS

Investment had been heavy in the late eighteenth century. A basic measure of investment was that imports of capital goods such as timber and iron rose more rapidly than imports of consumer goods in the closing periods of the century. During the war years from 1793 to 1815, apart from a sharp recession in investment in 1797 and 1798, capital formation continued at a high level. In this period, the great canals, the Royal and Grand, started their operations. New factory investment was at a high level too. Building flourmills reached a new peak with the largest mills in Ireland completed in 1814. Town growth was rapid in the early seventeenth century, and the major expansion of Irish towns and urban buildings culminated in 1815.

The investments boom slowed in 1815; as a result, prices fell sharply. The volume of exports between 1815 and 1820 fell. It rose further in 1821, but the value was still in decline. A deep economic crisis occurred in the spring of 1820. This crisis was the most severe in two decades. The main cause was falling prices, impelled by falling markets in the United Kingdom, where a depression hit in 1819. Grain, beef, and pork prices fell through 1819 and 1820. The unexpected crisis in 1820 contributed to monetary deflation. Since 1797, suspending payments caused a sharp rise in circulating notes. Circulating notes rose more sharply in Ireland than in the United Kingdom. To some extent, when agricultural prices rise more rapidly than other prices, the supply of money passively follows.

However, there was also an excessive creation of credit, encouraged by speculation. In late 1819 and early 1820, the Bank of Ireland restricted credit. Falling prices were already making merchants vulnerable; customers, suspecting the solvency of the banks, were eager to convert their claims against banks into cash and sought payment, not in local bank notes but in those of the Bank of Ireland. The bank carried out its policy of credit limit by lessening its rediscount of bills for other banks. Therefore, the banks could not get the notes their customers wanted, and many failed. The banking crisis began in Munster because of price increases due to wars. Thus, there was a rise in note circulation, but prices fell sharply after 1815.

Seven of the fourteen banks in Munster and Kilkenny failed. From a peak of £1.5 million in 1813, circulating private bank notes in the south fell to £400,000 in 1823.

Banking and Credit Crisis

Irish banks, like banks in other countries, started when individuals with surplus capital and economic resources wanted to manage their investments. Merchants were the ones that always created banks, because they could invest in banking, using some of the profit of their trade. In addition, land agents, who held cash from many property owners, wanted to use the money for a short term, for their own interest.

Bankers performed as follows:

1. They lend money on their security bills of exchange.

2. By selling and buying bills of exchange, they eased transferring money within both Ireland and England. A bill of exchange, drawn from another party in another centre, made up a claim to credit in that centre.

Merchants were eager to convert credits into cash by selling them to a banker. However, when merchants or agents had no credit in a centre where they needed one, they could buy a bill of exchange from the banker. In general, bankers handled much of the country's foreign exchange. Through their correspondents in the countryside, they handled the movement of money inland and within the country as well.

Dublin and Cork were the only extensive centres of banking. The growth of banking had been rapid in the 1720s. By the end of this decade, the number of bankers in Dublin had risen to six. Besides, the number of banking houses continued to grow in the prosperous years.

In the outset of the 1750s, eight banks were operating in Dublin, and more started their services in Waterford, Clonmel, Athlone, Belfast, and Galway. The number of bankers was small. More merchants became bankers themselves, which increased some banks openings. Irish people could buy a bill of exchange from a merchant as well as a banker. In addition, merchants were willing to buy bills because they had constant need of money in other towns. Some merchants provided these services extensively. A banker usually issued promissory notes payable to bearer. However, many merchants in Cork also issued promissory notes. This circumstance made it difficult to distinguish between a banker and a merchant in that city. In 1756, the failure of three merchant banks in Dublin and two in Galway in 1754–1755 caused the Parliament to pass a bill that outlawed bankers from engaging in foreign trade as merchants. However, the act did not restrict merchants from engaging in the issue of notes payable to bearer, if they did not describe themselves as bankers.

From 1759 to 1793, there were only four or five private banks in Dublin. Cork, Limerick, Waterford, and Belfast were the only other towns in which new banking businesses opened within the same period. Nevertheless, without issuing notes payable to the bearer, there were many merchants with whom private individuals lodged money and who performed banking services. The most serious financial failures, involving bankruptcies of merchants, always occurred after bad harvests. The rise in imports of grain, following the bad harvest of 1726, and the highest adverse rates of exchange experienced in the 1720s created the crisis, which resulted in a major banking failure in Dublin in 1727.

The huge grain imports after the disastrous harvest of 1744 reflected a prolonged control of credit during 1745.

The rise in grain imports in 1752 and 1753 led to the most serious crisis yet experienced. Dillons Bank in Dublin failed in early 1754. The crisis deepened even further by the spring of the following year: two more banks failed in Dublin in March 1755 and two in Galway. Following more bad harvests, another major crisis started in 1770–1771 with the bankruptcy of many merchants and the temporary closure of one Dublin bank.

These failures were not only due to bad harvests. Tight credit or widespread failure among merchants or bankers occurred in years when the balance of trade had contracted sharply and credit was severely lessened in weight. The exception to the association between a worsening balance and a financial crisis was the tight credit. This happened during the first half of 1767, in part the result of slower cash returns in linen, leading to the collapse of many business houses. Grain imports were high that year. Poor linen sales could also adversely affect the country's exports and so lessened the favourable balance. The bad years in the linen trade often preceded or followed years of poor harvests: a credit struggling to overcome one crisis needed a fresh one.

The huge fall in the sales of linen from 1772 through 1774 was a result of two years of harvest failure. Thus, the credit crisis of 1772–1773 began. The house of Colebrook in Dublin went out of business. In 1782–1783, linen sales fell sharply; prices at livestock fairs in the preceding autumn of 1781 had also proved disappointing. This was the beginning of the long credit squeeze of 1782–1784. Bad harvests in 1782–1783 made the situation more serious, and a major credit crisis affected the country's business life in 1784.

Most people believed the credit crisis of 1759–1760 and 1777–1778 was the result of bad linen sales. Sales fell in 1758–1759 and in 1759–1760. A severe crisis developed in the autumn of 1759, with bank failures in Cork and Dublin and widespread bankruptcy among business houses. The severe credit crisis of 1777–1778 began from a sharp slump in linen sales.

The crises in 1819–1820 and 1825–1826 were notable because of monetary deflation in Ireland. At this stage, the Bank of Ireland aimed for a policy of stabilising the exchange between Ireland and the United Kingdom. An act assimilating the Irish and English monetary units passed in 1825. English coins replaced Irish coins, and the parity of exchange began in 1737. Therefore, Ireland stopped having a separate currency. The same gold coin was the basis of the monetary system for both Ireland and England.

Banking was not the sole cause of Irish economic problem. The real problem was finding investment outlets.

In the eighteenth century, there was a large inflow of capital into Ireland, which helped to finance the rapid growth of the economy. The economic changes of the early nineteenth century lessened the attractiveness of investment in Ireland. Notable in the textile industries, but to a lesser extent in other industries, changing organisation and strengthened English competitiveness was reducing the range of paying outlets. Lacking outlets in Ireland, Irish capital was beginning to flow to the United Kingdom.

New Policy on the Irish Economy

Before becoming political independent, the Irish economy was influenced by the British economic policy. After Ireland became independent, its economy was driven by policies based on industrial protection, and these policies were considered by Sinn Fein leadership as the cornerstone of Ireland's economic development policy. However, in addition to these new economic policies, Ireland continued to seek financial support from the United States of America, an emerging economic power in the global economy.

In the beginning of the 1900s, the United States had surpassed the United Kingdom as the world's leading producer of iron, steel, coal, and textiles. According to McCormick (1989, p. 19), the increase of US power meant an ideological shift, away from protectionism to an informal imperialist programme of opening doors for US expansion. After World War I, Woodrow Wilson's administration extended US influence abroad. In his Fourteen Points Statement of 1918, Wilson called for global free trade and an end to colonialism. This was an unwelcomed development in Britain. Between 1920 and 1930, the idea of global free trade coincided with the attention of Irish republicanism. Southern Ireland was on the verge of successfully achieving political independence. The United States made incursions against European control of colonial resources. While America stopped UK plans to create a rubber cartel, US oil companies gained a foothold in the Middle East. Some US corporations preferred to cooperate with European powers to access their colonial resources, instead of backing government policies to break down colonial control. American society, mostly small miners, farmers, ranchers, and industrialists, favoured protecting US markets, while large financial firms and big industry wanted access to foreign materials and markets.

In a series of secret studies of American interests in the Great War, the Council on Foreign Relations (CFR) studied different scenarios in the peace process. They got help from top academics, businessmen, and political leaders. They set out plans for a postwar world economic order, under different assumptions depending on whether Germany won or lost. These plans included an international monetary system (IMF), the International Bank for Reconstruction and Development (IBRD), and an agreement on international trade and exploiting minerals (Council on Foreign Relations 1946). The CFR members dominated the executive agencies and postwar reconstruction bodies that would carry out the programmes (Block 1977; Shoup and Minter 1977; Wexler 1983; and Hogan 1987). The postwar goal of America was to create a trading strategy that would integrate European and Asian markets for its major industries. Thus, US trade patterns shifted to exports and imports in manufactured products, which would solve the problems of international supply and demand. US capital exports would finance and organise European recovery. The United States aimed to sell its industrial products to Europeans, who in turn would pay using colonial raw materials and money earned from colonial trade (Upgren 1940). Peripheral countries themselves became important consumers of US products. The trading system regulated foreign direct investment (FDI). Free trade opened the door to US capital exports and material imports. They had control of mineral reserves, using private US firms, which ensured an increase over time of such trade. The United Kingdom was a massive importer of surplus Western grain, meat, and dairy products. UK colonies, especially South Africa, India, Malaysia, Australia, and New Zealand, contained most of the raw materials needed by US industry. Europe as a whole became the main source of demand for American industrial exports.

Based on the above context, decolonisation simultaneously removed UK colonial controls and the most effective barriers to its colonies. Economic change in southern Ireland was ambitious, as the industrialising state's political and business elites hoped to use independence as a route to self-sufficient economy through industrialisation and agricultural progress. However, even though they succeeded, they created conditions that enabled Irish industry on foreign-led dependent development. This was the starting point where the Irish economy grew at the level of global trade. Instead of being self-sufficient, the Irish economy was under the influence of foreign investors and driven by foreign-owned exports.

Part II: Independent Ireland

Economic Policy

Ideas, knowledge, science, hospitality, travel—these are the things which should by their nature be international. Let goods be homespun whenever it is reasonably and conveniently possible and, above all, let finance be mostly national.

If I were an Irishman, I should find much to attract me in the economic outlook of your present government towards self-sufficiency.

—J. M. Keynes

The Irish signed a treaty with the United Kingdom in 1921. Under this treaty, Ireland became the Irish Free State, comprising thirty-two counties. In 1949, when twenty-six of those counties withdrew from the UK Commonwealth, six counties, known as Northern Ireland, remained part of the United Kingdom (even though with devolved government with limited jurisdiction from the Republic of Ireland).

As the Irish Free State, in the first years of independence, free trade continued with the United Kingdom, and economic

27

policy concentrated chiefly on raising efficiency in agriculture. The Irish government collected and transferred land annuities to UK commissioners of the national debt. Land annuities were annual repayments made by Irish farmers for money loaned by the UK government under the Act of 1921.

Despite the annuities transfer to the United Kingdom, Irish agriculture prospered, and over 98 percent of Irish exports went to the United Kingdom in 1923. Thus, the agricultural sector remained important for the economy of the Irish Free State.

The main change was the rise of small owner-farmers, former tenants who won the right to buy their land after the land wars. Where only 3 percent of agrarian workers owned land in 1870, 64 percent owned their farms by 1921. Three-quarters of farms belonged to family-owned holdings of less than fifty acres. Most of the land was in the hands of farmers who owned estates of more than 100 acres.

Manufacturing in the south was mainly brewing, distilling, and agricultural processing. According to the Department of Industry and Commerce (1933), net output was concentrated in drink and tobacco firms. Only 130 companies employed more than a hundred people. Many of the large firms like Guinness were subsidiaries of UK-based corporations.

Many industries grew throughout Ireland, even though Dublin had the highest concentration. Most manufacturers were artisans. Large firms wanted to continue free trade with the United Kingdom, and owners of small-and medium-sized firms favoured protection. This was because competing imports of shoes, clothing, and grain threatened their markets. Some large industries hoped that protection would bring new opportunities for profitable investment. Several coachbuilders lobbied the government for restrictions on car imports so they could assemble cars themselves (Jacobson 1977). The Irish labour movement supported industrial development through protection and the creation of a state industry. Thus, the greatest pressures came from the popular class.

Pressure mounted for a more nationalist economy and self-governance. In 1926, members of a moderate nationalist opposition, led by Eamonn De Valera, formed the Fianna Fail political party. In 1932, they won election by promising a vigorous programme for economic self-sufficiency and creating indigenous industry. After taking office, De Valera's government announced that it would stop paying annuities to the United Kingdom. Immediately, UK officials adopted measures to punish Ireland. The government imposed a 20 percent tariff on trade with the Free State. In turn, this prevented the United Kingdom from selling coal to Ireland. Since UK markets constituted over 98 percent of Irish exports, the tariffs were costly. This was the origin of the economic war between the two countries. In 1938, they signed an agreement to end the trade war. Under this settlement, Ireland paid the United Kingdom £10,000,000 to pay off its annuities.

During this time, lower capital started deepening, which became a huge problem. In 1945, Ireland had only five state companies. This included the Electricity Supply Board, set up in 1927; the Sugar Company, begun in 1933; Air Lingus, which started in 1936; Ceimici Teoranta, which opened in 1938; and Irish Shipping Ltd., begun in 1941. During severe stagnation in 1945, the Department of Industry and Commerce insisted that the industrial structure of this country grew based on private enterprise. The government felt that in general, the continued expansion and development of industry should belong to private individuals and groups (Kieran, Giblin, and McHugh 1988). In 1933, Ireland created the Industrial Credit Company, with an aim to underwrite new industrial projects and expansions. Irish nationalists sought industrialisation to reduce economic dependence on the United Kingdom. Cattle exports to the UK were the primary sources of foreign exchange, for industrial inputs, while export earnings gave farmers optional income to buy domestic products. The United Kingdom was hostile towards Ireland's infant regime, and the English recession threatened Irish development. Following English import quotas, Irish agricultural exports plummeted from more than IR£33 million to IR£18 million (Department of Industry and Commerce 1935). The Anglo-Irish trade agreement of 1938 restored trade relations with the United Kingdom; however, World War II caused the UK to again restrict its imports from Ireland. The Census of Industrial Production (Department of Industry and Commerce) shows that southern Irish industrial growth slowed during the war years (1939–1945).

AGRICULTURE

The structure of Irish agricultural production became progressively more pastoral in the second half of the nineteenth century. From 1912 to 1913, livestock products accounted for roughly four-fifths of the value of total output. The decline in the tillage share continued in the first period of independence, and by 1930, crops and turf accounted for only 16 percent of the value of total output. In the early 1930s, Ireland switched from agricultural policies to tillage. Ireland also started producing many foodstuffs. World War II raised the share of crops and turf to about one-third of total output by 1944. After the war, the relative tillage declined again. The beginning of 1985 showed a decrease of 12 percent of total. Cattle and milk increased their share, and by 1985, they accounted for roughly three-quarters of the value of total output. In 1930 and 1950, pigs, poultry, and eggs accounted for over one-third of the value of total output but declined to less than one-tenth of the total by 1985.

In general, a great proportion of agricultural production was part of larger farms, more specialised in dairying and beef and more capital-intensive. This change was a product of twenty-five years of faster output growth. However, the change brought a halt to Ireland's agriculture industry. While the number of small farms declined in some areas, a significant number of them continued to work in such environments. Thus, marginalisation rose in the poorest western parts of the country. Until the 1950s, these small farms survived on a stable subsistence basis. They consumed a significant proportion of their own produce without sale. They worked their land more intensively, with a higher output per acre. Nevertheless, from the mid-1950s, the pattern reversed; the high levels of productivity correlated with farm size. Only larger farms registered growth. Therefore, few of today's remaining small farms are viable. Their survival is dependent on the state's social welfare policy, though suitable policy measures could play a positive role in agricultural development.

The policies adopted in agriculture differed from those of pre-independence. Subsidies, import controls, and protective policies became important to Ireland's vision, which was to restructure the pattern of domestic production. These measures weakened Ireland's position in UK markets. The protection policies lessened efficiency but improved marketing. Irish farmers faced difficult conditions for much of the period from independence until Ireland's entry in the European Economic Community. The poor output-price environment contributed to keeping down Irish farm incomes, thus restricting both the means and the incentive to invest. The unfavourable output-price ratio gave farmers little incentive to increase productivity. Irish farmers earned the reputation of being erratic suppliers of goods that were sometimes inferior in quality. In 1961, the state set up a centralised Dairy Board (An Bord Bainne) to deal with marketing problems for dairy product. The main roles of the board were to improve marketing methods for dairy products and to develop export markets.

The main support for farm incomes was through output price subsidies, particularly butter and milk. Investment incentives and input prices subsidies stimulated higher productivity. Ireland government provided grants to drain land and other renovations through land project grants. In the 1950s, fertiliser subsidies increased on Irish farms. The government began to pay for categories of livestock, to increase their numbers. Introduced in 1954, by 1964 the state contributed heavily to the disease eradication programme, notably for bovine tuberculosis and for brucellosis in 1969.

Between 1950 and 1971, despite contributing to above policies to grow performances, the Irish real price did not improve. The sharp rise in the Irish real price started in 1973, as result of Ireland's entry in the European Economic Community. Irish agricultural prices went up to the levels prevailing in other member states. The rapid expansion in output brought the proportion exported up to 60 percent. In the 1980s, this expansion led to lower prices in Europe.

DECIDING ON THE IRISH INDUSTRY

In 1949, the Department of Industry and Commerce identified IR£60 million worth of imported products. The question is why Ireland did not invest to produce them in the country, thus creating 45,000 jobs. In 1951, Ireland gathered a list of foreign-made products. The list included plastics, ceramics, washing machines, vacuum cleaners, steel pipes, and paper. Local industry, however, did not provide leadership in investing in these products. The idea of the Department of Industry to concentrate their efforts in limited fields was wrong. Ireland has depended on outside imports since 1951. The idea of "erecting industry on a basis of private enterprise" showed less returns in Ireland economy. The numbers of protected manufacturing firms had grown by 35 percent between 1931 and 1947. The domestic bourgeois did not have political power, as a class, to counter the rising change. Most new corporate owners concentrated on their individual interests rather than their class interests. These corporate owners set up industrial branch associations to petition the government about tariffs and other policies related to their businesses. Instead of drawing capital together, these associations competed among each other: "Dublin versus Cork, City versus County, Large versus Small, Producers versus Suppliers, etc." (66 Business Conference 1967, p. 48).

In the 1960s, their average membership was just twenty to thirty companies. In this association, for example, the flour milling industry simply functioned as cartels whose main role was to limit entry and to control production and prices. On the other hand, local chambers of commerce continued to support free trade instead of protection. The leading Irish industrial journal dismissed the large Dublin Chamber, created under Cromwell, as "intermediaries and agents for foreign goods." The Federation of Irish Manufacturers (FIM) began its work in 1932. The main goal was to ensure that "industrial development shall keep the hands of Free State" (O'Hagan and Foley 1982, p. 15), and membership was restricted to Irish-owned firms. The FIM's political power lay in its ability to enact legislation, from the control of Manufacturers Acts to anti-worker employment provisions. During the 1930s and 1940s, all major ministers attended FIM annual conferences and dinners, and a liaison group from the Department of Industry and Commerce attended all its meetings. In the 1950s, because of economic stagnation, attendance at FIM's meetings fell from hundreds to dozens. Members began to complain that the government did not pay "sufficient regard" to its suggestions.

Despite problems in the industrial promotion to create jobs, the industrial working class had grown. Industrial workers raised from 13.4 percent of employees in 1926 to 21.8 percent in

1951. Trade union membership quadrupled in the same period. Industrial workers supported protectionism, but their consistent pressure for higher wages and social programmes continually brought them into conflict with the state.

Further, the state proposed changes to the system of industrial promotion. However, a conflict emerged between financial conservatives and expansionists. The expansionists proposed laws to attract new export-oriented projects. The Department of Finance opposed that policy as state-centred. Domestic capital aligned with conservatives against government regulation, leaving attracting export-oriented industry as the only alternative. In 1947, the Department of Industry and Commerce tried to create an "industrial efficiency bureau" to combat excess profits taking. Companies that did not respond adequately would face a court of inquiry. If companies did not follow the bureau's directives, the state could seize their excess profits. If employment played a major part, the minister could seize a company's assets and run it as a state concern.

Reaction to these proposals was immediate and hostile, from the conservative bureaucrats to the Irish capital. The FIM claimed that the proposed legislation would do away with the right of private enterprise. It requested a meeting with the Taoiseach to discuss a "tendency" among ministers to imply that manufacturers had "controlled themselves of unreasonable and excessive profits at the expense of the buying public" (Federation of Irish Manufacturers 1949). In the face of such hostile mobilisation, the government dropped the proposals.

Further, in 1948, there was a proposal to set up an Industrial Development Authority (IDA), which shows how the defeat of government law attracted new industry. The draft bill on the IDA envisaged that it would start schemes to attract industry. The IDA was to have powers to call on witnesses and documents from private industry. Conservatives strongly opposed such a body as "a dangerous machine for the exercise of corruption." The FIM and the chambers of commerce opposed granting the IDA powers to look into business. The Drapers Chamber of Trade called such powers "an unjust interference with the liberty of the individual." The five directors of IDA were prominent company directors and representatives from the FIM and the Federated Union of Employers. Despite the splits with Irish capital, those who sat on the IDA were mostly expansionists and outwardly oriented businesspeople. The IDA was to become the single most important institution charged with attracting new industry to Ireland. Thus, IDA became the Irish government's inward investment promotion agency, accountable to attract and to develop foreign direct investment in Ireland. In this regard, if consultations with the Irish capital were selective, the working class did not engage in decisions about creating and staffing the IDA. In early 1949, the secretary of the Congress of Irish Trade Unions wrote to the Minister for Industry and Commerce to protest the composition of the IDA and the lack of consultation with labour about its creation. When a delegation from the congress later met the Taoiseach to complain about the IDA, he informed them of the "danger" he saw in trade union proposals for consultation and participation in decision making. From this point, indigenous industry changed to a body newly dependent on the interests of foreign-owned companies.

RETHINKING THE AUTONOMY OF IRISH INDUSTRY

I should ask if Ireland is a large enough unit geographically, with sufficiently diversified natural resources, for more than a very modest measure of national self-sufficient to be feasible without a disastrous reduction in a standard of life which is already more to high.

—J. M. Keynes

Before Ireland achieved its independence, the south was an unfavourable industrial milieu, while the north was the more favourable industrial place. Irish industries invested in building Belfast, Northern Ireland. However, while Belfast was a key trading centre, the southern Ireland industries were insufficient to promote market development (Lee 1973, p. 16). Lack of resources in southern Ireland did not boost industries until the Marshall Plan began in 1948. Thus, instead of boosting indigenous Irish industries, the south of Ireland's economic growth got help from foreign investments.

Between 1948 and 1951, the United States carried out its European Recovery Program (ERP), also known as the Marshall Plan. The programme was begun by the Economic Cooperation Act of April 1948. The aid was distributed to recipient countries under the Economic Cooperation Agency (ECA). In the beginning, the Irish Finance Department opposed receiving Marshall Plan aid. However, the Minister for External Affairs, Sean McBride, hoped European Recovery Program funds would help increase the state's role in investment. Without aid, he argued, "Ireland will [be] practically unable to get most of the requirements needs from the dollar areas." In 1948, Ireland accepted the aid and joined the Organisation for European Economic Cooperation (OEEC). During negotiations to join the OEEC, Americans made it clear how they expected the Irish government to use the aid. They insisted that Irish draw up acceptable spending plans. The Americans also asked that aid "help in national development purposes of a productive nature and not [be] invested in United Kingdom and other securities." This statement targeted the Department of Finance, which wanted to use the aid to redeem government debt (Fanning 1978, p. 419). In a direct intervention in Irish economic affairs, the ECA chief suggested that Ireland should set up an export corporation and give the United States access to Irish natural resources, "directly or indirectly," to raise the country's earnings. These pressures to gain free entry to Ireland for its corporations came at the same period as a new ECA programme. US corporations in Europe wanted their investments to come back in their country under transfer of profits using their currency, the dollar. Only thirty-eight US companies took advantage of the programme. This was a prelude to "the massive post-war rise in United States corporate investments in Europe and other areas" (Wexler 1983, p. 88).

The United States applied more subtle pressure on Ireland. The chairman of the board of National City Bank in New York told T. K. Whitaker, a principal officer in the Department of Finance, that the United Kingdom would probably get no more aid because Americans considered their nationalisation programme and welfare state "obnoxious." US taxpayers, he claimed, were "much averse to social tax policies in the United Kingdom." The UK regulated foreign capital too much, he continued, adding that "American investors would wish to have control over enterprises in which their capital was invested." High corporate taxation in the United Kingdom made investing "almost impossible."

By contrast, in Ireland, there was a system of grants to industrial enterprises for building new factories and buying machinery. Originally suggested by the ECA as a way of using Marshall Funds, it became the Underdeveloped Areas Act of 1951 and was extended throughout Ireland in 1956. During an interdepartmental ERP committee meeting, it was suggested that Sean McBride openly admitted using US pressure to win support for his department's spending programmes over Department of Finance objections. In a speech to the Irish Institute of Bankers, an American journalist noted that Marshall Aid did not consider "the basis of needs, but on a basis of merit" (McGilligan1948). Aid now depended on efforts to make currency convertible, to liberalise trade, and to integrate the European economy. The United States demanded "universal, nondiscriminatory, free trade" in Europe. Under US pressure at the end of 1949,

OEEC members had to remove quotas from at least 50 percent of their imports in agricultural products, raw materials, and manufactured goods. This changed to 60 percent in September 1950, and 75 percent in February 1951. Ireland consented because it would lose Marshall Funds if it declined to conform.

In 1955, the quota limit moved up to 90 percent. At this phase, internal pressures against free trade mounted to their highest. In early 1955, the Irish government tried to use US aid to finance its development schemes. In the end, US and European pressure forced Ireland to move from protection to free trade.

In 1949, T. K. Whitaker tried to warn of the dangers of using Marshall aid to fund new spending programmes. He divided state payments into "productive" and "social" units, claiming that social spending was excessive. He also insisted that high taxes discouraged private investment. Nevertheless, the government responded to his analysis as too restrictive and "gloomy," saying that all sides should be "discussing a dynamic economy not a static one"!

Marshall Funds ran out in 1951, and Ireland's balance-of-payments shortfall grew. The Central Bank reported that the government was spending more than the nation could afford. At this point, the Department of Finance gained support for its austerity policies. Therefore, in 1952, austerity budgets abolished food subsidies and cut social services. The Department of Finance drew up strictly balanced budgets against wage demands. Austerity programmes continued through 1955. The Department of Finance added an intensive campaign for higher interest rates to "encourage saving" and "put a brake on new borrowing." The Central Bank also refused to cover the government's borrowing, and the Secretary of Finance told the Taoiseach that the governor of the Central Bank had lost confidence in the government. In this situation, the parliamentary secretary accused the department of "conditioning" the government to follow policies that were "contrary to the good of the community."

In 1956, Taoiseach John Costello announced a series of industrial grants, tax breaks for exporters, and other incentives to industry. The Industrial Grants Act of 1956 extended capital grants for new manufacturing projects throughout the country. Finance Acts of 1956, 1957, and 1958 gave 100 percent profits tax relief to exporters. In addition, Ireland joined the International Monetary Fund (IMF) and the World Bank in 1957. It also removed the Control of Manufacturers Acts, which restricted foreign investments. In 1958, the Industrial Development Act removed limits on foreign investment and gave the IDA extended powers to seek out and encourage foreign investment.

As a result, the legitimacy of Irish investment, begun during the 1930s as the engine of southern Irish economy, ended. Taoiseach Garret Fitzgerald claimed that

> the sense of failure of economic policies predisposed Irish people almost overnight to favour new departures; and this mood of rejection extended to the policy of protection. ... So rapidly were public attitudes on this issue reversed that those who had an interest in maintaining industrial protection and who had hitherto secured the support of public opinion on this issue found it impossible to resist this movement. (1968, pp. 54–55)

The economic crisis deepened in 1957, as the conflict among Irish investors over foreign investment and free trade continued. In the beginning of 1959, the *Journal of Irish Industry* wrote:

> Today our Irish government is favouring the foreign investor more than ever before. Huge free grants of the Irish people's money went to those coming in here to set up industries, a

good portion of such free grants being from funds received in taxation from Irish manufacturers. We regret the Federation of Irish Manufacturers is almost completely silent on this matter. (*The Journal of Irish Industry* 1959, pp. 3–4)

At FIM's annual meetings, some members spoke against government incentives to foreign industry; however, others argued that local industrialists should expand, instead of opposing foreign industry. This conflict became so strong that OEEC proposed creating a European Free Trade Area (FTA) in 1956. The president of FIM opposed the FTA, suggesting that bilateral trade agreements would be better for Irish industry. Nevertheless, his members split on FTA. Some FIM delegates argued that free trade could cause Irish small businesses to shut down. Others argued that experience of free trade was "no criterion of what will happen in the new Free Trade Area" (*The Journal of Irish Industry* 1957, pp. 39–45).

Finally, at a conference on the proposed FTA in early 1957, manufacturers expressed fears of international economic retaliation if Ireland did not join the scheme. The president of the Cork Regional Group of the FIM said that Ireland should join the area because it was "economic suicide to stay out." During the second conference on free trade in 1958, instead of opposing free trade, delegates argued about gaining government support to prepare for foreign competition. Some asked for low wages and lower taxes to help them survive free trade.

From 1974 to 1981, multinational companies grew rapidly. These multinational companies included pharmaceutical, healthcare, and electronics companies from the United States. In 1979, the IDA's managing director claimed that the foreign electronics sector was "recession-resistant" and that electronics employment would grow to 25,000–30,000 by 1985 (Killeen 1979, p. 14). Nevertheless, according to IDA employment surveys in 1985, fewer than 19,000 people got jobs in electronics, and less than a quarter of those were in highly skilled categories. The recovery of employment began at the end of the 1980s because of rising multinational investments. Around this time, exporting multinational companies received about 40 percent of grants, while indigenous industry received 25 percent (Fogarty 1973). As a result, employment in indigenous industry fell. Jobs losses amounted to 35,000 and were particularly high in the textile, clothing, and food sectors. A survey of new Irish companies suggested that "the biggest major external catalyst for these entrepreneurs was domestic house market, through the products that went into houses rather than construction work" (Rothey 1977, p. 56). In 1963, 28 percent of manufacturing companies employing over 500 people were foreign owned. This proportion grew to 48 percent in 1973 and 57 percent in 1986. In 1973, seventy-one United Kingdom companies received grants to retool, and they employed an average of 190 workers, compared to 39 in indigenous Irish industry. Total employment in UK-owned companies in 1973 was more than 33,000, and this number fell below 15,000 by 1990.

Except in 1979, employment in UK-owned companies fell in every year. Total employment in multinational companies fell from 11,933 in 1973 to 3,531 in 1986. The number of companies fell from sixty-eight to thirty-seven. Thus, the decline of foreign companies in Ireland in the 1980s caused a decrease in Irish employment, which confirms that the engine of Irish economic growth was foreign-owned companies. The decrease in Irish employment in the 1980s rebounded as result of rising foreign investments in the 1990s. These companies engineered the rapid Irish economic growth in the 1990s (the so-called "Celtic Tiger"). Irish economic growth was dependent on the health of foreign-owned companies and their willingness to invest in Ireland.

Beginning in the 1980s, Ireland's industrial policy underlined some of the weaknesses of its reliance on foreign corporations.

Among these weaknesses was transfer pricing, whereby foreign-owned corporations inflated the value of output in the Irish economy, to benefit themselves of the state's low taxes and manufacturing profits. The extent of capital repatriation by foreign-owned corporations grew 2.8 percent of gross domestic products in 1979 to over 17 percent in 1998 (OECD 1999, p. 28). According to Walsh (1996, p. 77), the effect of dominating foreign corporations in Ireland is evident in the "particularly sharp decline in investment by Irish-owned firms, despite their improved profitability. The largest and dominant Irish companies opted to geographically diversify, rather than trying to expand into new products in Ireland" (Ibid., p. 85).

Further, in studying Irish industry, O'Riain observed the following:

> It took the economic crisis of the 1980s to delegitimise the Industry Development Agency's IDA's role as the sole bearer of the task of Irish industrial transformation. It was into this restricted institutional space that alliance of Irish technical professionals and the previously marginalised "Science and Technology" state agencies stepped to support Irish industry. (2000, p. 181)

In addition to IDA, in 1994, Ireland established Forbairt, an agency to develop Irish industry. Policies were shifting towards greater selectivity in grant giving and a greater focus on marketing, technology, and Irish industrial companies (Ó'Connell 2000). According to O'Malley (1998, p. 35), there were signs of "a substantial and sustained improvement in the growth performance of Irish industry." This happened from 1987 to 1997, across a wide range of industrial sectors and indicators, such as output, employment, spending on research and development (R&D), and export as well as profitability. O'Malley argues that the improvement was more than a response to stronger domestic demand conditions and indicated an open improvement in competitive performance. The value of Irish manufacturing plants increased by 9.6 percent in 1995, 4.3 percent in 1996, and 4.7 percent in 1997, compared to 2.7 percent in 1994 (O'Sullivan 2000, p. 271). Moreover, he finds a strong increase in research and development expenditure by Irish-owned manufacturing enterprises in the 1990s (Ibid., p. 273).

In an analysis of start-ups and closures in the manufacturing industry from 1986 to 1995, Foley and Hogan (1998) find the size of firm at start-up did not show any significant increase. However, the numbers starting up in modern subsectors increased, while those starting up in traditional subsectors declined. Foley and Hogan clarified that start-ups in the Irish software subsector showed a marked increase, from 336 in 1993 to 561 in 1997. Thus, the software sector was an example of success in Irish industry in the 1990s. Employment grew from 3,800 in 1991 to 9,200 in 1997. Over this period, the value of exports increased from IR£61 million to £365 million. Research and development spending in nominal terms increased from IR£4.6 million in 1991 to £34.6 million in 1997. Ireland spent twice as much on research and development in its foreign-owned companies (O'Sullivan 2000, pp. 273–74). This extra expenditure on Irish foreign-owned companies shows that foreign-owned companies got favourable treatment over Irish companies.

Engine of the Irish Economic Growth

After the failure of the economic strategy mainly based on agriculture and protectionism policy, from the 1950s to the 1970s, the Irish government's economic policy ran on the use of grants and tax cuts to encourage export-oriented products. The liberalisation of Irish markets, which was its third strategy, became attractive to foreign manufacturing enterprises (Kennedy et al. 1988, p. 236). The government's strategy to attract foreign manufacturing to come and invest in Ireland was designed to boost the Irish economy. According to O'Grada (1997, p. 114), at the outset few foresaw the rapid growth of the foreign sector, but direct foreign investment in Irish industry soon became the cornerstone of government policy. The remarkable transformation of the Irish economy between the late 1950s and the early 1970s may largely be credited to the presence of multinationals. Kennedy identified different stages of foreign direct investment. The first stage of FDI began when protectionism against importation to home markets increased. The second stage happened through the late 1950s and 1960s, when many firms produced, for export, fairly labour-intensive products such as clothing, footwear, textiles, and plastics, in addition to light engineering. Finally, machinery, pharmaceuticals, instruments, and electronics sectors became predominant (Kennedy et al. 1988, p. 240).

Afterwards, Ireland set up an export-processing zone in Shannon, County Clare. Many foreign firms were attracted by the package of investment incentives, which encouraged them to export what they produced according to Sklair 1988 (quoted in Kirby, 2002). By 1973, foreign-owned companies accounted for roughly one-third of all manufacturing employment. By 1983, there were nearly 1,000 foreign companies in Ireland, and they had invested over £4 billion. Half of these companies came from the United States, one-eighth from the United Kingdom, and around one-tenth from Germany (O'Grada 1997, p. 115). While manufacturing output grew between 1958 and 1973 at 6.7 percent per annum, employment in manufacturing grew at 2.4 percent (O'Malley 1992, p. 34). Exports grew from 19.4 percent in 1960 to 41 percent in 1978 (O'Malley 1989, pp. 69–92).

On the other hand, the agriculture measures helped to preserve small farmers through providing direct income support and through encouragement of rural industrialisation to provide off-farm employment. The Underdeveloped Areas Act of 1952, allowing grant aid for new industrialisation, gradually changed into a policy of regional balance through which the state sought to reduce regional disparities for job seekers (O'Tuathaigh 1986). The problem, however, was that instead of trying to promote a policy of industrialisation based on local linkages through processing agricultural inputs, the Irish government chose to encourage multinational companies to locate in rural areas. This met with a measure of success: by 1978, 59 percent of foreign firms in Ireland were located in designated areas (Breathnach 1985, p. 178). However, by the very nature of this type of industrialisation, its weak linkages to local suppliers meant that it formed an enclave (Ibid., p. 187). There was hope that Irish industry would expand and prosper under free trade; "the combined effect of free trade and the upheavals caused by the oil crisis was far more devastating than most people had imagined" (Kennedy et al. 1988, p. 241). There was no further employment growth in this sector from the mid-1960s to the end of the 1970s, and in the 1980s, employment fell sharply. Although the Irish firms concentrated in domestic markets, they declined as domestic demand fell in the early 1980s (O'Malley 1992, pp. 35–36). The greatest decline became obvious when foreign competition intensified, for example, in chemicals, metals, textiles, clothing, and footwear firms (Kennedy et al. 1988, p. 242).

Most Irish industries dominated in subsectors involving either basic processing of local primary products, like the food industry, or activities such as construction, cement making, paper, and packaging. That was their industrial strategy, which was explained in the Telesis Report in 1982. The report found that "attention shifted to the international competitiveness of the whole industrial sector rather than merely its export unit." In 1992, the Culliton Report appeared to highlight the same results. The Culliton Report recommendations led to dividing the Industrial Development Authority into separate agencies for foreign-owned firms and Irish industries. These changes in industrial policy played a major role in a "remarkable turnaround" in the fortunes of Irish industry (Ó'Connell 2000).

Despite the policy change, from the early years of the 1990s, foreign-owned companies in Ireland emerged as the main engine of the economy. According to Newman and O'Hagan (2008, p. 214), Ireland has the most FDI-intensive manufacturing sector of all countries in Europe. Thus, even though Ireland became sovereign, it emerged as the main market of foreign-owned companies. Over the past five years, the United States accounted for more than half of all the inward investment in Ireland (Crooks 2010). There are more than six hundred US companies in Ireland, employing 100,000 people (Hennessy 2011). American companies invested $165 billion in Ireland, more than in Brazil, Russia, India, and China together (Crooks 2010).

US companies investing in Ireland include Boston Scientific, CITI, Intel, Pfizer, and Medtronic. Boston Scientific set up in Ireland in 1994 and is the largest medical device company in Ireland. It employs 4,900 people. According to IDA Ireland (2011), CITI was the first international financial institution to receive research, development, and investment financial support from the Irish government. To date, CITI invested €62 million in research, development, and investment projects in Dublin and created a Centre of Excellence for developing products and processes (CITI's EMEA Business). CITI employs 2,000 people. Intel settled in Ireland in 1989. It is the largest semiconductor chip maker and has a 75 percent share of the microprocessor market. Its largest customers are Hewlett-Packard and Dell. Intel employs 5,715 people. Over the past years, it has invested €7 billion and provides 9,050 jobs in the Irish economy (IDA 2011). Intel exports $2 billion from Ireland yearly. It paid €1.4 billion in taxes to the Irish government over the last ten years (IDA 2011). Pfizer started its operations in Ireland in

1969 and employs over 1,650 people. It produces human and animal medicines and healthcare products. Its total capital investments in Ireland exceed €7 billion (IDA 2011). Medtronic employs 2,000 people and develops technologies for managing cardiovascular and cardiac rhythm diseases. In addition, Ireland is home to eight out of the top ten pharmaceutical companies in the world; currently, there are roughly 20,000 people employed in the pharmaceutical sector in Ireland (O'Leary 2011).

A low corporate tax rate (12.5 percent), a well-educated workforce, and membership in the European Single Market created a growing Irish economy. The Celtic Tiger became the backdrop of foreign-owned trade, mainly exports by US-owned companies. Intel, Dell, Pfizer, and Hewlett-Packard are some of the foreign manufacturing companies responsible for 90 percent of Irish exports (McArdle 2005). In addition, the life sciences sector created $52 billion worth of exports in 2009 (O'Leary 2011). These companies are significant contributors to the success of the Celtic Tiger (Finfacts 2011). The US boom of the 1990s also helped. The main cause of the collapse of the Celtic Tiger in 2008 was a systemic crisis in the US economy. Since Ireland's independence, the largest part of economic growth depended on America, and the other way around. More goods exported from Ireland came from American-owned companies. In other words, the largest part of Ireland's trade originated from foreign-owned firms, not indigenous companies.

THE EFFECT OF FOREIGN COMPANIES ON THE IRISH ECONOMY

The decision to invest in a foreign country relies on securing an advantage in any market division. Ireland does not control corporate decisions, neither by direct political action nor by market instruments like taxes. Instead, Ireland attracts foreign investors by promising low taxes, low wages, and other incentives like grants. State agencies such as the Industrial Development Authority relied on good relations with foreign investors to identify opportunities for indigenous entrepreneurs. Indigenous companies could lose competition from foreign corporations, so Ireland's solution should be to set up a national programme that protects local industries.

This was the main reason Forbairt was created in 1994. Its major objective was to help indigenous companies to grow. In addition, Forbairt advised and helped start-up businesses. The organisation decided to include exportation and training owners and managers of private companies. Enterprise Ireland took over these responsibilities from IDA. Enterprise Ireland's role is to help and advise indigenous companies about markets strategies. In 1996, out of 2,667 indigenous firms, only 174 were subsuppliers to foreign corporations in the Republic of Ireland (for example, materials and packaging). Ruane (1999) cites data that point to backward linkages of foreign firms rising from IR£627 million in 1990 to IR£1,490 million in 1996. The proportion of raw materials purchased locally by foreign corporations increased from 18.8 percent in 1990 to 19.1 percent in 1996. The rise in local purchases was an effect of rising corporate output in Ireland. Thus, corporations bought more of their inputs from other corporations' subsidiaries in Ireland. For example, Dell bought Intel's processors. Forfas, Ireland's policy advisory board for enterprise, trade, science, technology, and innovation (1997), estimated that two-thirds of "local buys" in the electronics sector consisted of one corporate subsidiary buying from another.

Enterprise Ireland found that in the 1990s, foreign corporations highlighted globally integrated unit supplies, which were beyond the capacity of most Irish producers and essentially cut them out of the market for supplying corporations (Breathnach and Kelly 1999). Despite that, Irish industry concentrated their efforts in the software sector. Foreign corporations bought a substantially smaller share of their material supplies in the year 2000 than in 1990. The growing software sector in 1994 and 1996 became the real Irish success story, the place where "the new breed of entrepreneurs—the Celtic Tiger"—was best represented (Lucy 1996).

Software exports from the Republic of Ireland generated IR£3 billion from 1993 to 1995, an increase of roughly 60 percent. By the year 2000, the Republic of Ireland was the second largest exporter of software, behind the United States. According to O'Riain (1999), the rise of indigenous software in the 1990s had only indirect ties to the influx of foreign computer firms. However, 82 percent of Irish software companies had no alliances with corporations. While in 1997, 108 foreign-owned software corporations employed 9,100 people, 571 indigenous software firms employed 9,200 people. From 1993, foreign software employment had doubled from 4,448, while indigenous employment doubled to 4,495. Foreign-owned corporations continued to increase their share of manufacturing employment output and exports from 1987 to 1995, against the share of indigenous industries. This trend became evident since the 1960s for output and exports (O'Malley 1989, 1998) and since 1973 for employment (Ruane and McGibney 1991).

According to Fitzgerald (2000, p. 38), the proactive industrial strategy of Irish policymakers was central to the long-term development of a strong industrial base. This policy focused on attracting foreign corporations to settle in Ireland. In the 1990s, this policy succeeded in attracting to Ireland some of the world's leading corporations in three main sectors: healthcare, pharmaceuticals and medicals devices, and software and electronics (as well as international financial services). The first sector included 150 foreign corporations that employed 25,000 people in Ireland by the end of 1990s and formed 20 percent of the country's exports. The second sector included foreign industrial and "was at the heart of rapid transformation of the country economic and prospects. It employed 28,000 people, with 30 percent of country's exports" (Sharry and White 2000). The finance sector employed 27,000, mostly from foreign corporations.

From 1987 to 1992, inflows of FDI to Ireland increased from an annual average of $615 million to $838 million in 1994, $2,618 million in 1996, and $6,820 million in 1998. US investment made up more than 80 percent of the overall flows in Ireland in the later years of the 1990s (O'Sullivan 2000, pp. 263–64). The writings on Irish industrialisation must capture the development activities of foreign corporations in Ireland's economy (see Ruane and Kearns 2001). According to O'Riain's (1997, p. 195) analysis of the software sector, Ireland become an operations hub, developing its own information technology agglomerations. Also, encouraging foreign corporation to find product development in Ireland competes against those companies' need to hold control and so is likely to have limited success. In 1990, O'Sullivan studied research and development spending and expenses on indigenous inputs; there was an increase in activities that had a greater developmental impact on the Irish economy. R&D spending by foreign corporations increased from 0.7 percent of gross output in 1991 to 2 percent in 1997. O'Sullivan inferred that R&D intensity was flat or declined in the sectors most heavily dependent on foreign activities (2000, p. 269). Even though higher levels of activity by foreign corporations led to an increase in spending in absolute terms in the Irish economy:

> It is certainly not possible to identify a trend towards a deepening of linkages between foreign and indigenous companies at least through the analysis of the collect behaviour of foreign companies' local buys; if anything, in fact, the evidence points in the opposite direction. (Ibid., p. 270)

Furthermore, she pointed out:

> Ironically, as Ireland has become more integrated with the European Union in macroeconomic terms, the microeconomic structure of Ireland's industrial economy has changed to more closely resemble a region of the United States. The country's dependence on the United States, especially in sectors that are notoriously volatile such as electronics, means that Ireland is highly exposed to the risk of significant fall in recent United States economic liveliness. Although evidence of a significant deepening of the relationship between foreign corporations and their Irish bases might well be grounds to temper such a view, the analysis of R&D spending and linkages . . . does not provide support for such an interpretation. (Ibid., p. 283)

THE ORIGINS OF IRISH RECESSIONS

To understand the origin of recession in the Irish economy, first it is necessary to explore the strategies that led the Irish government to influence economic growth after independence.

The Irish currency was still linked to the UK currency. The Irish government's economic policy relied on the agricultural sector, and Irish markets stayed in the United Kingdom. Thus while the Irish economic policy increased from agricultural products to exports, its main markets remained in the United Kingdom. The second strategy was introducing a policy of protectionism in 1932 to encourage Irish self-sufficiency and reduce imports from the United Kingdom. The third strategy was the economic development proposed by T. K. Whitaker and published by the end of 1957. The idea of the plan got its footing from opening the Irish economy to international trade. In other words, Whitaker's economic strategy originated from liberalising Irish markets and attracting foreign direct investments. The final strategy started when Ireland joined the European Economic Community in 1973.

As discussed earlier, the first and second strategies were unsuccessful in stimulating Irish economic growth. According to Mjoset (1992), the failure of Ireland to diversify its total dependence on Britain had serious outcomes for its economic performance when compared to other small European countries. Therefore, despite independence, the Irish government found it impossible to deviate from the UK markets. Thus, Ireland's dependence on the United Kingdom was unchanged. The second strategy created a series of decisions to encourage the growth of Irish indigenous industry. It also pushed Ireland to support economic growth by reducing its dependence on the UK economy. However, these strategies fostered a new way of rethinking about Irish economic growth. All these strategies created a keystone to successful growth. Despite its independence from the United Kingdom, the Irish economy had a positive review from powerful countries, such as the United States, Germany, and France. Contrary to the myth, Irish economic growth depended on the economic growth of powerful countries, and the other way around.

Therefore, this means the origin of the Irish economic crisis in 2008 was not the crash of the Anglo-Irish Bank. The fundamental origin of the financial crisis came from the historical structure of Irish markets and policies. The crash of the Anglo-Irish Bank pointed to problems in the Irish economy, but it was not the sole origin of the economic crisis. The Irish economic crisis did not come from closing down of Irish domestic investments; it originated from closing down foreign investments in Ireland, especially from the United Kingdom and the United States. In other words, the Irish economic recession came from the collapse of the global economy, the collapse of the US economy, and the collapse of the UK economy. According to Honohan (2009, p. 1):

> It was always to be expected that Ireland would be particularly exposed to a global downturn, considering the large contribution of exports to Gross Domestic Product (GDP) and [the] vertical integration of much of Ireland's manufacturing into the global production chains of major multinational firms. These were characteristics which, when combined with the steady growth in world trade, contributed to a sustainable boom for over 15 years. Now they had gone into reverse.

> By mid-2008, the Irish export sector had to cope with a sharp slide in the value of sterling—the currency of neighbouring Britain, still a major trading partner. Indeed, the sudden fall in sterling left even the domestic retail disclosed of suddenly low prices.

Despite Ireland's fiscal austerity during this economic downturn, the growth of the Irish economy was always depending on foreign investments. During the recession of the 1980s, the Irish government reacted by increasing taxes on labour and consumption to reduce budget shortfalls. However, even though the deficit fell by a significant percentage, the debt to gross domestic product continued to climb, and by 1984, further tax increases could no longer solve Ireland's fiscal situation (Lane 2000). The amassed debt was 116 percent of gross domestic product by 1986 (O'Leary and Considine 1999). To bring Ireland's budget under control, Charles Haughey's government applied austerity measures to cut government spending: 6 percent on health, 7 percent on education, and 7 percent on the military. Agricultural spending fell 18 percent, and roads and housing fell 11 percent. In addition, through early retirement, other incentives, and a voluntarily jobs cut, public sector employment fell by nearly 10,000 jobs (Jacobsen 1994, p.

177–78). The government abolished the environmental agency Foras Forbatha and the National Social Sciences Board as well as the Health Education Bureau and regional development organisations.

In 1988, government reduced spending by 3 percent and cut capital spending by 16 percent (*The Economist* 1988, p. 9). The cuts in government spending got Ireland out of its fiscal crisis. After eliminating the primary deficit in 1987, the debt-to-GDP ratio started falling sharply from its peak. By the end of 1990, government debt was less than 100 percent of GDP (Honohan 1999, p. 81). However, in addition to the Irish government's austerity measures, the origin of the economic recovery was inflows of foreign direct investment (Murphy 2000).

The Credibility of the Irish Currency

After independence, the Irish Free State kept the currency that it inherited from years in the United Kingdom. According to Honohan (1999), it was the introduction in 1926 by the new government of a series of distinctively Irish tokens that began to raise some doubt or ambiguity about the status of Irish currency. Though the new coinage represented more a gesture of national pride than of economic policy, the Irish pound became an issue.

To fix the future of the Irish pound, in 1927, the Irish government appointed a commission under Willis Parker of Columbia University in New York. In 1942, the Parker Commission recommendations led to a new unit of account: "sterling." They also created a standing Currency Commission to introduce Irish legal tender currency notes against the sterling receipt. Consolidating existing private bank notes into a single parallel currency became part of the seigniorage it taxed. The

Central Bank of Ireland began operations in 1943. It did not lend to the banks or the government. In addition, it made no efforts to influence the trend of credit through regulations or interest rate actions. Its main policy intervention was one of outspoken critiques of the "constantly increasing scale of state spending and local authorities." This came to light in the bank's 1950–1951 report. The Irish pound, linked to the sterling, delivered a stable environment for trade in both the United Kingdom and Ireland. Thus, the reason of preserving the link with the sterling was continuing close economic relations between the two countries and the need to keep international confidence in the Irish pound. Nevertheless, in the 1970s, high inflation in the United Kingdom failed to preserve price stability in Ireland. The relationship between sterling and the Irish pound misled all Irish strategic thinking.

For most of the period, the wholesale money market available to the banks in Ireland was coming from London. From the 1960s to the early 1970s, Irish authorities agreed to London interest rate increases, which automatically affected Irish interest rates. Because Ireland had experienced inflation averaging 15 percent between 1973 and 1979, it became a priority to detach the Irish pound from sterling and link it with the European Monetary System (EMS), which was based on Germany's deutschmark. Ireland joined EMS in 1979 (McArdle 2005). The decision by the Irish government to link the Irish pound with EMS was again a sign to forget their national monetary policy rights, for the interest of the exchange rate and trade. Ireland's change in monetary policies was aimed at giving confidence to investors. So the Irish market broke links with sterling and joined the European Monetary System. The next step was to convert the Irish pound to the Euro, a common currency. The main reason that drove the Irish government to abandon its rights to sovereign monetary policy was fear for inflation from the United Kingdom.

While there were some reasons to price stability for national currency to Irish economy, it was obvious that linkage to the currency of large foreign countries was more useful to the local Irish economy. It was smart for Ireland to convert its currency into the Euro, because a common European Union currency simplified price stability in trading and exchange in exports. The Euro currency gave its members free movement to invest in the Eurozone without any charges. These advantages, however, could have increased Ireland's benefits or caused losses. For example, in the 1990s, Argentina's currency converted to US dollars at a fixed rate of one peso per dollar. Thus, when the US dollar appreciated, Argentina's commodities exports declined. The variations in the value of the currency to which the national currency of a country links can produce unexpected volatility. Before his resignation in 2001, Domingo Cavallo, the Economy Minister of Argentina, announced a move to a currency board with an anchor defined as a basket of one half dollar and one half Euro (Frankel 2003).

Similarly, Lithuania, while keeping a currency board arrangement, responded to the difficulties created by the late 1990s appreciation of the dollar by switching from a dollar anchor to the Euro (Frankel 2003). On the other hand, the currency of Thailand had no formal rigid links to the US dollar; the Thai Bath came under attack following adverse capital market events during 1996–1997. The Thai Bath depreciated, and the government could not intervene. Between July and October 1997, the Bath fell by as much as 40 percent (Lee 2011). Then in July 1997, the Thai government had to make their currency float before accepting an International Monetary Fund bailout.

The overvalued US dollar also caused currency crises in Mexico in 1994, Korea in 1997, Russia in 1998, Brazil in 1999, and Turkey in 2001. Now, these countries already abandoned their links with the US dollar to free-floating exchange. Under a free-floating currency, a country has monetary independence, so when real growth is temporarily low and unemployment is high, the central bank can use quantitative easing measures to stabilise or increase economic growth. A worsening in the international market for a country's exports usually leads to a fall in the value of its currency. According to Frankel (2003), some analysts say that Australia came through Asia's 1997–1998 crisis in fairly good shape because its currency was free to depreciate automatically in response to a decline in exports markets. Like Australia, Canada and New Zealand are commodity-exporting countries with floating currencies that automatically depreciate when the global market for their commodities is weak. Most countries around the world have different currencies; exchange volatility could be difficult for exporters from small, open economies.

Foreign exchange risk is difficult to control because the price of exportable goods comes from terms of foreign currency. Today, there are many discussions about flexibility in exchange rate (Edwards 2002; Eichengreen 1994; and Frankel 1999, 2003). The advantages to fixed exchange rates are a commitment by the central bank to favourably affect the expectations of multinational investments. The main job of a central bank is to convince the international capital flows that they need not be afraid of depreciation or inflation. A small open economy like Ireland's depends on international trade, so it is a privilege for Ireland to integrate in the Eurozone. This means the decision to break the Euro currency is a disadvantage for Ireland but not for large countries like France or Germany. The 2008 crisis in the Irish financial system did not happen because Ireland is a member of Eurozone or because of a Western recession. The 2008 debts crisis in Irish banks came from imperfect Irish domestic policies in the housing markets; they were the cataclysm of government strategic planning. Irish government supported over-investments in Irish housing markets, which was the demon of the crisis. Thus, the credit crunch in the Irish financial system started with excessive loans in the housing market, from the government-housing plan. Some argued the cause of the financial crisis and long-lasting recession in Ireland originated from bank deregulation. However, even though the rule was necessary, Irish bank laws alone could not stop the recession in Ireland. The crisis in the Irish financial system was the child of the historical structure and governance of Irish markets.

THE NEED FOR CHANGE

Since 2008, Irish families have been upset with Irish politicians' ideologies. They complain of losing their daughters, their sons, and their community as well as their way of life. Irish people—young people, adults, and families—continued to emigrate. They distrusted Irish economic strategies that did not improve markets. They had enough of watching their politicians maintaining the status quo, trying to comfort the Irish economy with the same economic policies.

The general elections of 2011 raised the hope of the Irish people that change would take over the policy of status quo. However, we are still far from changing Irish economic strategies that started in 1948. The government has failed to stimulate the economy from Irish-owned companies and Irish enterprises; the Irish economy continues to suffer from the closure of foreign direct investments.

After the failure of the Irish government to strengthen indigenous companies, the Industrial Development Authority was created in 1948. The IDA became the single most important institution capable of enabling Irish economic growth. The institution's job was to attract foreign direct investments in Ireland. From the 1950s, IDA became the Irish government's inward investment promotion agency, in charge of developing ways to stabilise Ireland's imports and exports. Thus, Irish indigenous companies became dependent on foreign-owned companies. Today, exportation of Ireland commodities is under foreign direct investments based in Ireland. This underscores the dependence of Irish economic growth on foreign-owned companies. The high Irish unemployment is the effect of closing down foreign-owned companies. Instead of improving the efficiency of Irish companies and Irish enterprises, the government continues to focus on foreign-owned companies. Most Irish economists continue to argue the economy is suffering from politicians unable to create the proper strategies. The Irish economy would be sustainable if the government policies of job creation improved the efficiency of Irish enterprises.

Despite the Action Plan for Jobs 2012, which considered supporting Irish indigenous companies, more efforts continue to focus on foreign direct investment. Since Ireland became independent from the United Kingdom, young people and adults continue to leave the country, because politicians are unable to create economic policies that can sustain the economy and create jobs.

While the Great Famine increased Irish emigration, there were Irish emigrants before 1845, with some estimates of 1.5 million Irish emigrants crossing the Atlantic in the period from 1815 to 1845. Lack of job creation is a major determinant of Irish emigration. In brief, there have not been significant improvements in the Irish economy since setting up the Irish Free State in 1922.

Irish Working Abroad Expo 2012

At this jobs fair, more than fifty companies across the healthcare, construction and farming sectors offered jobs in Canada, Australia, New Zealand, and other countries.

According to the *Irish Independent* (2012), thousands of people were turned away from a Jobs Expo in Dublin in one weekend, and demand was huge in Cork. Hundreds of people from all over Munster queued for entry into Cork's Silver Springs Moran Hotel, hours before it opened. People were reported to have slept in their cars to ensure that they got in.

One couple who live in Wexford had travelled to Dublin for the Working Abroad Expo there, but they did not get in. David Walsh, organiser of the Expo, said he was overwhelmed by the turnout:

> "I feel humbled and heartbroken at the sheer numbers that have turned up today, and I apologise to the people who had to queue in the rain. My only advice is that if you didn't make it today then all the relevant information is available on our website," he told the *Cork Independent*. "Employers are over here to recruit. They are readily available. They are not going to stop recruiting."

The photos below show long queues formed in Dublin as thousands of Irish headed to the Working Abroad Expo 2012. The exhibition provided information on visas, emigrating, and job opportunities overseas.

Photo: Laura Hutton/Photocall Ireland, Dublin 2012

Photo: Laura Hutton/Photocall Ireland, Dublin 2012

Photo: Laura Hutton/Photocall Ireland, Dublin 2012

Photo: Laura Hutton/Photocall Ireland, Dublin 2012

Photo: Laura Hutton/Photocall Ireland, Dublin 2012

Brother and sister Jack and Katie Dunne, aged 22 and 21, visit a Canadian stand at the Working Abroad Expo at the RDS. Photo: Laura Hutton/Photocall Ireland, 2012

Karen Martin (27) and Darren Zeltner (23) visit an Australian stand at the Working Abroad Expo at the RDS. Photo: Laura Hutton/ Photocall Ireland, 2012

Thousands also attended Working Abroad Expo in Cork.

Cork Independent, **2012**

Curtin.B.H(2012) 'Thousands queue to leave Ireland. Cork Independent, 08 March 2012. <http://corkindependent.com/stories/item/7915/2012-10/All-abroad> Accessed 4 April 2012.

Part III: How Irish Politicians View Irish Governance

The main idea for part three of this book came from a chapter of *The Naked Politician*, "Your Local T.D. Will Never Seem Quite the Same Again" (Honnon 2004, pp. 4–167) and from *Republicanism in Ireland: Confronting Theories and Traditions* (Honohan 2008, pp. 2–103). This chapter tries to explore how the Irish politicians view the Irish governance.

> Dáil[1] Deputies, or some of them, dragged themselves back to work yesterday after their long Christmas holidays. But only in a manner of speaking. They dragged themselves back into Leinster House, but not to do the work for which they are paid, the work allocated to them by the constitution. ... Leinster House has almost become irrelevant to the public business carried on by the civil service and state agencies. (Irish Independent 2007)

> The Oireachtas[2] is an archaic body, governed by rules and regulations that were already outmoded in the 20th century,

---

[1]   House of Deputies.
[2]   National Parliament.

never mind the 21st. The Dáil has become little more than a talking shop, with very little real work being done in the chamber. (Sherlock 2008)

The . . . minister [is] the corporation sole of the department. That is to say the legal personality is the minister and department is no more than an extension of that personality. (Barrington 1980, p. 31) This means that the ministers are accountable to the Dáil for actions of their civil servants.

I believe that successful governance of a country is critical to economic sustainability. All depends on good ideas and more rational alternative economic strategies that increase job creation. If we want the Irish economy to be sustainable, we should think how to better govern or conduct our daily public administration business. Therefore, accountability in Irish institutions is imminent, because when an error happens in Irish public administration, it is hard to find who is responsible for that mistake. Therefore, we need executive accountability within or outside our institutions.

Inside the Irish Cabinet and Parliament

"Oh, what pitiful people."
Dr Noel Browne

According to Browne (quoted in Honnon, 2004) in Irish governance, "you have the politician who is obsessed with the business of getting to the top and staying there, and the politician who is interested in changing society." Thus, there are two different aspects to Irish governance. Browne believed that some Irish politicians immersed themselves in politics in an effort to fill an emotional void from the sudden death of their fathers. Browne distinguished between those who were driven by emotional needs from those who, like himself, had an ideological commitment.

> They are going different ways, really, because one is faced with compromise if he wants to survive, and the other knows that if he compromises he cannot achieve his objective. Moreover, my experience of Irish politics is predominantly of the former. After a short time in the cabinet observing these people and the way they would capitulate to every whim of the hierarch, I began to feel "Oh, what pitiful people." (Honnon 2004, p. 4)

Dr Moosajee Bhamjee, a former member of the Irish Parliament (and a member of the Labour Party), said:

> There is no debate in the Irish Parliament. You come, give your speech, and go away. I used to enjoy Question Time. Nevertheless, even that got a bit boring because they were reading from these ready-made speeches. In addition, as a government backbencher, you could not question your own minister. People think you are a TD [member of Parliament] and you can ask for something and the ministers give it to you. In fact, it was hard to meet some ministers. ... It was boring to be in the Dáil. To be sitting there trying to ring government departments. There was tedious work involved as well. People have this impression that the life of a TD is always exciting. However, 90 percent of it is boring. You have to show your people that you are doing something. You have to shout the loudest. You also have to make sure that you get in the doughnut. (Honnon 2004, p. 120)

Michael D. Higgins, the current president of the Republic of Ireland, said that "the official system really felt that you couldn't get people to change their burning habits without grant." He says that a minister's reluctance to agree to amending legislation started back to the irritation of their officials, who warned strongly against granting a change. Mary Harney, a former Minister for Health, recalls that "was the culture. That was the way the system thought you solved problems. You must pay people to change behaviour." She acknowledged that even though the fundamental statute governing Irish public administration gave the minister all the responsibility in a department, an Irish civil servant can have more power than a minister. The system in the departments is more used to saying no to a new idea than yes.

According to Harney,

> you will get all the reasons why it should not happen. That is a fact. Minister must be up early in the morning to meet the challenge. While ministers arrive in their offices with little or no in depth knowledge of the brief, you have to spend a fair amount of time reading the brief. When it comes to policies, you need to know that you are going to be debating with people who knew an awful lot more about it than you did. Moreover, importantly, they know all players. Some of them have been at it for ten or twenty years. They may have a particular perspective or they may just have become accustomed to doing things in a certain way. (Honnon 2004, p. 152)

In 1983, Garret Fitzgerald appointed Nuala Fennell Minister of State with responsibility for Women's Affairs and Family Law Reform. In brief, she would work in the Department of the Taoiseach and the Department of Justice. In the Department of Justice, it was the tradition that the secretary general of the department would introduce Fennell to the department. Fennell described her first meeting with secretary general of Department of Justice:

> We went in and sat down, having tea. It was as if I was a clerk they were thinking of employing and I was being interviewed.

> He was a charming man and he had a good rapport. … He said, "Well, that's nice now, Minister, we'll send you over any port that comes here for you."
>
> I had just been appointed into his department, and here he was dismissing me! I said, "Oh, no, no, no. I need an office here." The Secretary General then explained that this would a problem, as he did not actually have any spare office space in the department. They didn't want me. I was a load of trouble. They hadn't to cope with a women's libber and all that went with that. It is civil service politics, and they want to retain their control. (Honnon 2004, p. 153)

Most serving and formers ministers agree that civil servants often block positive initiatives in a knee-jerk response to the dangers of change; Fitzgerald accepts that ministers are at the mercy of senior civil servants (Honnon 2004). His long experience has convinced him that departments have their own policies, to which they are strongly committed. "The idea that they're neutral is nonsense," he said.

When Michael D. Higgins first became minister in 1993, he frequently had a good laugh in discussions with Dr Noel Browne at how ministers were given the runaround by their civil servants:

> There are ways of defeating a minister. When you arrive at a minister's office for the first time, there will be this long sideboard of files. And the senior servants will say to you, "Minister, the files . . ." He gives a little royal wave to demonstrate how it would be done. You must say to the secretary general at that stage: "Which one do you think won't wait until next week?" At which time you will notice that all the files will disappear. Civil servants love the ministers who know nothing about their brief. You could be completely at

their mercy. You are at an immense disadvantage. (Honnon 2004, pp. 156–158)

Being minister in five different departments, Ruairi Quinn, a labour TD and current Minister for Education, said:

> It takes an awful long time to learn to be a minister. The first time around, you feel that you are going to do everything. A lot depends on your training. Very few people who end up at ministerial level in politics have had any managerial experience. The nature of becoming an elected person is such that you really cannot be a mainstream management type. Very few people have worked at a middle-management level in a big organisation. So learning management techniques and expertise on how big organisations work is something that you have to acquire on the hoof. … You have to say to yourself these things are worth doing and if I get more than fifty percent of it, it is still worth doing. Nevertheless, if I have to trade to a certain point, then it is not worth doing. You are not going to work below a bottom line. Does everyone work by these standards? It depends on what you are there for; if you simply want to be on the pitch, there is not a bottom line. (Honnon 2004, p. 154)

Charlie McCreevey, a former Minister for Finance, took a view that many people start out with the best of intentions, but by the time you crawl your way up, you are beat.

Furthermore, Fitzgerald acknowledged that the constant tension between doing the right thing and the need to be reelected can make it difficult for people to act as well as they should. There is a sense of public service. Nevertheless, over time it is very wearing. Over time, it weakens people's resolve.

> There are always these choices between the popular and the right thing. You cannot always do the right thing regardless

or you would never get re-elected. Therefore, there is compromise. What you have to do is not do wrong things, and do enough popular things that aren't wrong, to be able to do some of the good things. ... I think most people try to do the right thing but the pressures on them of public opinion are such that they very frequently don't. (Honnon 2004, p. 167)

In contrast with the above discussions, a retired secretary general of the Department of Finance took the following view:

Only those who have worked close to ministers have any ideas of the many demands on their time. One indication of the limited amount of time which a minister can devote to the affairs of his departments is the difficulty that the official head of the department [the secretary] and his senior colleagues experience in obtaining a meeting with him. Perhaps this difficulty is accentuated in the Department of Finance, whose minister is subject to unusually varied pressures; it is certainly not a problem of personalities since the difficulty does not vary much with different ministers. (Collins and Cradden 2001, pp. 54–59)

INSIDE THE IRISH DEPARTMENTS

In early days of Ireland's independence, Arthur Griffith expressed that it would be a much more difficult task to put an end to favouritism and family influence in appointments under local bodies in Ireland than to drive the British Army from the country. What happened under the old regime was that in each rural district every position worth having went to the members of two or three families. ... A candidate, no matter how highly qualified or widely experienced, had little prospect of securing an appointment if he or she were not related by birth or by marriage to one or other of the big three or four or five who ruled the Corporation, Council, Union, or Asylum Committee. (Lee 1989, p. 162)

Today, recruitment and promotion in administration services are based on merit. Thus, personnel selected for posts in the administration services must have both understanding and merit to do the work.

However, even though meritocracy is the right way to recruit, Ireland still needs to implement equality in public services. In other words, even though serious problems in Irish public administration did not start from favouritism, there needs to be a transformation.

The situations within the Irish cabinet are indications of serious problems in the Irish public administration. If we need a sustainable economic growth, it is necessary to change the current system administration in departments. Because the departments decide most national strategies, malaises in the services of departments affect all services. Therefore, a dysfunction of government departments is an indication that all services in the country are dysfunctional, because they control dysfunctional services from their departments. For example, in 2005 the Department of Health established the Health Service Executive (HSE). The HSE replaced the eleven regional health boards, which were linked to local councils. However, because of the dysfunction in services in the Department of Health, instead of giving responsibility to the HSE for controlling the functions of health services, the power over health services was transferred and centralised under the control of the Minister of Health. This dysfunction in the Department of Health led to the death of many children in HSE care. In her response in 2010 about the death of children, Mary Harney, Minister for Health in this period, never indicated who was accountable for those deaths. So neither the Department of Health nor HSE was accountable (see O'Toole 2010, pp. 51–52).

Moreover, the Health Information and Quality Authority (HIQA) found a number of "practice deficiencies" in the region during a wider investigation into foster care in seven HSE regions in Dublin and Cork (Smith 2010, p. 1). Additionally, the HSE said that over the past five years, cases of misdiagnosed miscarriage were "very rare" in the Irish hospitals. However, about a dozen women reported carrying dead babies. Despite that, the HSE declined to answer queries about its scan policy (Donnellan 2010, p. 1). Furthermore, a shortage of consultant radiologists at Tallaght Hospital and dysfunctional management at the facility led to approximately 58,000 X-rays going unreported at the hospital between 2006 and 2009. Tallaght Hospital also denied that 30,000 letters were unopened by general doctors. There were other examples underlining the same anomalies in various departments.

Furthermore, in 2011, the revelation that a sum of €3.6 billion was erroneously counted twice by the Department of Finance highlighted the fact that there are serious problems in Irish departments.

How Irish Political Parties Understand Ireland

Before signing the Anglo-Irish Agreement on 15 November 1985, Charles Haughey contended that the Irish republicanism to which his party, Fianna Fail, gave allegiance was "the political embodiment of the separatist rational tradition that is central to the freedom and independence of the Irish nation" and that this required adherence to the 1916 Easter proclamation; the 1919 Declaration of Independence; Articles 1, 2, and 3 of the 1937 Constitutions; and the 1949 Dáil Declaration against the partition of Ireland. In this context, in July 1986, Tánaiste and Labour Party Leader Dick Spring felt obliged to reaffirm his republican credentials, indicating that "the essence of that republicanism is uniting Irish people," while tracing its philosophical development "through Tone and Emmet to the Young Irelanders, through Parnell and Connolly."

In 1998 at Fianna Fail Ard Fheis, Taoiseach Bertie Ahern accepted that the Fianna Fail conception of republicanism was "perhaps too narrow in the past" and that "true republicanism has been about building, sustaining, and developing successful Irish parliamentary democracy." At the Humbert Summer School in August 1998, just days after the Omagh bombing, Ahern stated that "republicanism is about moving on, neither handcuffed to our history, nor heedlessly fugitive from it." Seamus Brennan, the minister with responsibility for overseeing the 1798 commemorations, argued that republicanism "is always and only about creating a society free of inbuilt constraints to the achievement of the full potential of all its citizens." In this respect, John Hume asserted that "true republicanism is not about flags and emblems. It is about establishing inclusive political institutions to which all sections of society can give their allegiance. In a genuine republic, all citizens can play a full role in determining the future of that society." At the annual Wolfe Tone Commemoration in Bodenstown in 2000, Ahern recognised aspects of republican heritage within each of the political parties, including the "constitutional republican" credentials of the SDLP, and argued that Fianna Fail's mission "is to develop and strengthen throughout the island modern democratic and constitutional republican traditions."

In September 1999, Ruairi Quinn, the leader of Irish Labour party, outlined his "ten pillars for a real republic." Central to his prescription was "a constitutional guarantee of fundamental social and economic rights for every citizen; full employment and guaranteed participation in a vibrant enterprising economy for every worker. ... [And] the active promotion of a pluralist and tolerant civic culture to ensure equal rights for all minorities."

For Fine Gael, in 2003, Senator Brian Hayes, a spokesman on Northern Ireland, highlighted republican themes underpinning the actions of the Cumann na nGaedheal governments from 1922 to 1932. Parliamentary democracy in the fledgling Irish state was established; the constitution of the Free State was enacted; civilian control over the army was secured; a new, unarmed police force was founded; and an independent permanent civil service, open to all on a meritocratic basis, was created. Fundamentally, the transition of power from Cumann na nGaedheal to Fianna Fail in 1932 confirmed these achievements. Hayes made the following observation on Irish republicanism of 1916:

> The Proclamation of 1916 was a revolutionary document that all Irish people could subscribe to. Republican principles must be at the heart of all political parties in a republic, however the real dividing point between parties comes not from republicanism, but whether a party is Socialist, Social Democratic, Green, or nationalist in perspective. That is ultimately where the difference lies. The reality is that those who founded this state came from various political and social backgrounds. It was clear that one thing above all else bound them together: the demand for independence. There was always a real division amongst those who fought for our independence, and the idea that one single agreed position on social issues was accepted is a good deal wide of the mark. (Honohan 2008, p. 101)

Michael McDowell, of the Progressive Democrats, has several strongly expressed interventions on the meaning and legacy of republicanism. He has also identified the importance of socioeconomic issues, arguing that "the values of a republic are based upon the maintenance of healthy tension between the civil, political, and economic rights of the citizen, on the one hand, and the aspirations of the community as expressed through a majority, on the other." This creative tension "depends fundamentally on the creation of a system of civil and political fundamental rights, and upon the functioning under the rule of law of democratic institutions to discharge legislative, executive, and judicial functions, and upon a deep seated individual and communal commitment to the resolution of difference by reference to democratic and liberal principal."

Moreover, McDowell has a highly state-focused analysis that centres on existing constitutional structures as well as a measure of political expediency. Additionally, he stated that Ireland was an independent sovereign democratic republic and that the Irish constitution contained the framework of that independence, that sovereignty, and that democracy. He highlighted that Article 9 of the Irish Constitution described "loyalty to the State" as a fundamental duty of all citizens and that election to Dáil Eireann was confined to citizens. He emphasised that the powers of government in the state were the exclusive monopoly of the organs of the state established under the constitution, that the sole power to raise a military or armed force is vested in the power of the administration, as justice is vested in the courts. He concluded:

> The provisions make it clear that no person who owes an inconsistent loyalty to any other body or group has a moral or constitutional right to seek election to Dáil Eireann. No person who owes a loyalty to any armed or military forces other than those maintained by the Oireactas has the moral or Constitutional right to seek election to Dáil Eireann. A vote for a candidate in Dáil Eireann who owes no loyalty to the State, or who subjugates that to the state to loyalty to a paramilitary organisation, is a clear and unequivocal breach

of our fundamental duty as citizens to give our loyalty to our independent, sovereign, democratic republic. (Honohan 2008, p. 101)

Gerry Adams, the leader of Sinn Fein, identified inclusiveness and equality as core to republican concerns for citizens in Ireland, stating that the members of his party

want a national republic, which delivers the highest standards of services and protections to all citizens equally, guaranteeing parity of esteem and equality of treatment, opportunity, and outcome. The republic Sinn Fein wants to build requires an accessible and responsive democracy, recognising and upholding basic human, civil, and political rights. It would promote economic equality through the exercise of social and economic rights. It would accept that these rights are not only indivisible, but in the interest of all. (Honohan 2008, p. 99)

Furthermore, in a speech in 2006 commemorating the events of 1916, Ahern expressed:

Citizenship cannot be delegated or outsourced. Citizenship comes with duties as well as rights. . . . In this republic, we are citizens, not subjects. And it is as citizens that we remember our past, reconcile our differences, and renew our hope for the future. Our civic duty calls on us to look beyond our purely private roles and rights as consumers to our active roles and responsibilities as citizens. Active citizens shape strong societies. The more we involve ourselves in shaping our society locally, the more our society nationally will reflect and meet our needs. Society is not abstract. It does not belong to others. It is the sum of our actions and our choices as citizens. (Honohan 2008, p. 102)

In the above discussions, all political parties emphasise the rights of citizens and their role in society. And they underline how the participation of all citizens could shape their society. However, their emphases are less on how they can sustain Ireland's economy, which itself can eradicate Ireland's socioeconomic problems.

Conclusion

THE FATE OF THE IRISH ECONOMY

Before Ireland's independence, UK markets were the main outlets for Irish trade, which took exports such as beef and pork; as result, UK policies became the main driver of Irish markets. Irish markets were regulated by UK policies, and the Irish economy was limited by the UK's interest within the global economy. In this way, while industries in the south of Ireland were insufficient, those in the north of Ireland were developed; Belfast was a more favourable industrial milieu and main trading centre. As an example, while industries of cotton in the north of Ireland were increasingly mechanised, southern Ireland weaving was still done in homes and in small weaving sheds. Moreover, despite low weaver wages, which meant that cloth from southern Ireland was affordable, the Irish markets in southern Ireland were unstable. And the markets were never developed, because its supply of yarn was unstable and because Irish weavers did not have enough capital. At this stage, Irish weavers were not in the position to mechanise the southern Ireland industries of cotton. Instead of mechanisation or innovation, the southern Ireland industries were sustained by low-cost labour.

Independence from the United Kingdom was the occasion for Ireland to develop domestic policies that could improve both Irish markets and Irish industries. However, the Irish government had mainly continued with pre-independence policies. Government created conditions that enabled Irish industries to depend on foreign-led economic growth. Irish markets and industries largely continued to be driven by foreign direct investments (FDI) and foreign-owned exports. According to Mjoset (1992), the failure of Ireland to completely break its dependence on the United Kingdom had serious consequences for its economic performance when compared to other small European countries.

In the first years of independence, Irish trade continued with the United Kingdom, and economic policy chiefly dealt with raising efficiency in agriculture. Industrial sectors in southern Ireland were mainly brewing, distilling, and agricultural processing. The policies adopted in agriculture differed from those of pre-independence; the emphasis was on the use of subsidies, import restrictions, and protective policies with a vision to restructuring the pattern of domestic production. But Irish farmers faced difficult demand conditions after independence. Although there were improvements in Irish agricultural policies from 1950 to 1971, real improvement began after Ireland's entry in the European Economic Community (EEC) in 1973. Improvement in Irish agriculture included the centralised marketing board, An Bord Bainne, established in 1961 to deal with marketing problems for dairy products and to develop export markets.

Because of the failure of Irish economic strategies, mainly based on agriculture and protectionism, new policies were based on the use of grants and tax reductions for export-oriented products. Nevertheless, the government was not successful in developing indigenous companies. Therefore, in 1948, the government established the Industrial Development Authority (IDA) to attract foreign direct investments. The IDA was to become the only institution charged with attracting new industry in Ireland. In other words, the Industrial Development Authority became the Irish government's inward investment promotion agency, accountable for attracting foreign direct investment. In addition to the attraction of foreign manufacturing enterprises in Ireland, the Irish government established an export-processing zone in Shannon, County Clare. In 1994, to support indigenous companies, the government set up Fobairt. The role of Forbairt was to advise start-up businesses and provide training for owners and managers of private companies. Today, the national programme is run by Enterprise Ireland, which also advises indigenous companies about marketing their products.

However, despite the effort of the Irish government to support indigenous companies, the attraction of foreign direct investments became a keystone to stimulate Irish economic growth. At this stage, however, the failure of Ireland to boost its economy from local companies continues to make the Irish economy suffer from decreased foreign direct investments. In other words, high unemployment in the Irish economy is largely caused by lower foreign direct investments in Ireland, and vice versa. Furthermore, most politicians think that the export-led growth will resume and Ireland will regain its prosperity. This is a short view, which fails to recognise the failures in Irish economic growth. The Irish economy needs to be more dependent on domestic enterprise than foreign-owned companies. In other words, 90 percent of Irish exports should come from Irish enterprises, not just foreign direct investments based in Ireland. We need a change in Irish economic strategy; otherwise, the Irish economy will remain unsustainable.

CREATING A SUSTAINABLE IRISH ECONOMY

I believe that we need effective institutions. Effective institutions play an important role in a country's economic prosperity, and they are accountable for effective economic strategy.

In this respect, a sustainable Irish economy needs successful Irish-owned enterprises and small businesses. Moreover, increased supports in Irish-owned businesses are needed because foreign direct investments in Ireland are driven by competitive rationality rather than the country's long-term economic growth. When share price in markets fall, the foreign-owned companies close down and move to countries where share prices are raising. Foreign-owned companies are better for employment in the short run.

The failure of Irish institutions to develop Irish markets can be resolved by a set of effective policies that relies on research training programmes, which can identify products and services needed in global markets. In this context, improving professional training in engineering and developing informal links between higher and technical education to support research in enterprises is a key for Irish economic growth. Furthermore, training programmes for people from disadvantaged backgrounds and displaced workers are also important. Ireland needs a market based on the services economy, not manufacturing. Nowadays, services are the main drivers for economic prosperity in the developed countries, because improvements in the business services increase competitiveness. For example, enhancements in transportation and communication technology have reduced the costs of transporting merchandise and lowered factors of production. Irish transport services and communication still need to be developed.

Above all, maintaining the security of people's lives is a core principal of productivity and progress. A decrease in business productivity is caused by a decrease in the country's active population. At this stage, Ireland needs to set more policies that improve the integration of all nationalities, native and migrant. Emigration is a consequence of a country that is unable to create strategies in relation to economic integration. When a country cannot offer productive opportunities to its people, they will move away, in search of a country that allows them to be productive. Moreover, people abandon their home country because they have no freedom of communication by capital, property, or security. In addition, a country that cannot integrate its people economically will cause them to emigrate. This is because when economic policies fail repeatedly, highly educated people will earn low incomes and businesses will earn low profits, thereby causing them to move where they can earn high income and high profits. The sustainability of the Irish economy needs a system of governing that facilitates performance in departments and local administration services, as well as increases investments in services. Ireland needs to devise a successful economic policy.

Bibliography

Agnew, J. H. (1994), *The Merchant Community of Belfast, 1660–1707.* Belfast: Queen University.

Alchian, A., and B. Klein (1973), "On a Correct Measure of Inflation." *Journal of Money, Credit and Banking,* pp. 173–191.

Aldous, R., and N. Puirsell (2008), *We Declare: Landmark Documents in Ireland's History.* Quercus Publishing Plc.

Barnard, T. C. (1979), *Cromwellian Ireland: English Government and Reform in Ireland 1649–1660.* Oxford University Press.

Barrington, T. J. (1980), *The Irish Administrative System.* Dublin: Institute of Public Administration.

Bernanke, B., and M. Gertler (1999), "Monetary Policy and Asset Volatility." *Federal Reserve Bank of Kansas City Economic Review,* Fourth Quarter, pp. 17–57.

Bernanke, B., and M. Gertler (2001), "Should Central Banks Respond to Movements in Asset Price?" *American Economic Review,* May, pp. 253–57.

Black, W. (1957), "Cyclical variations in the linen industry," in K. Isles and N. Cuthbert (eds.), *Economic Survey of Northern Ireland*, appendix G.

Block, F. (1977), *The Origins of International Economic Disorder*. Berkeley: University of California Press.

Caplan, B. (1956), *A Case Study: The 1948–1949 Recession*. NBR.

Cohen, M. (1990), "Peasant differentiation and proto-industrialisation in the Ulster countryside: Tullylish, 1690–1825." *Journal of Peasant Studies*, pp. 413–32.

Collins, N., and T. Cradden (2001), *Irish Politics Today*, Fourth Edition. Manchester University Press.

Considine, J., and E. O'Leary (1999), "The growth performance of Northern Ireland and the Republic of Ireland, 1960 to 1995," in N. Collins (ed.), *Political Issues in Ireland Today*. Manchester University Press.

Council on Foreign Relations (1946), *The War and Peace Studies of the Council on Foreign Relations, 1939–1945*. New York: Harold Pratt House.

Crotty, R. (1966), *Agriculture: Its Volume and Structure*. Cork University Press.

Cullen, L. M. (1972), *Economic History of Ireland since 1660*, Second Edition. Billing & Sons Ltd.

Culliton, J. (1992), *A Time for Change: Industrial Policy in the 1990s, Report of the Industrial Policy Review Group*. Dublin: Stationery Office.

Department of Industry and Commerce (1935), *Shipping and Trade Statistics 1934*. Dublin: Stationery Office.

Donnellan, E. (2010), "All GP referral letters are opened on receipt and processed according to speciality." *Irish Times,* March 12, p. 8.

Donnellan, E. (2010), "HSE to review misdiagnosed miscarriages in last five years." *Irish Times,* June 10, p. 1.

Dunnan, N., and Pack, J. (1991), "How to survive and thrive in the recession of 1991." Orlando, FL: Nova Southeastern University.

Edie, C. A. (1970), "The Irish Cattle Bills." *Transactions of the American Philosophical Society,* pp. 1–66.

Editorial (2007), "Welcome back, deputies." *Irish Independent,* January 25.

Eichengreen, B. (1993), *Reconstructing Europe's Trade and Payments: The Europeans System.* Manchester University Press.

Eichengreen, B. (1996), "Institutions and economic growth: Europe after World War II," in N. Crafts and Gianni (eds.), *Economic Growth in Europe since 1945,* Cambridge: Cambridge University Press, pp. 38–70.

Eichengreen, B., and K. Mitchener (2003), "The Great Depression as a Credit Boom Gone Wrong." Working Paper, Department of Economics. Berkeley: University of California.

Ellison, T. (1989), *The Cotton Trade of Great Britain.* London: Wilson.

Fabricant, S. (1972), *The 'Recession' of 1969–1970*. UMI.

Fanning, R. (1978), The Irish Department of Finance 1922–1958. Dublin: Institute of Public Administration.

Federation of Irish Manufacturers (1949), *Annual Report*. Federation of Irish Manufacturers.

Ferritter, D. (2001), *'Lovers of Liberty'? Local Government in 20th Century Ireland*. National Archives of Ireland.

Fisher, I. (1930), *The Stock Market Crash—And After*. New York: Macmillan.

Fitzgerald, G. (1968), *Planning in Ireland*. Dublin: Institute for Public Administration.

Fogarty, M. P. (1973), *Irish Entrepreneurs Speak for Themselves*. Dublin: Federation of Irish Manufacturers.

Forbairt (1996), National Software Directorate Irish Software Industry Survey 1995: Results. Dublin: Forbairt.

Forfas (1997), "Optimising purchasing linkages in the Irish Economy," mimeo. Dublin: Forfas.

Foster, R. F. (1988), *Modern Ireland 1600–1972*. London: Penguin.

Foster, R. F. (2007), *Luck and the Irish: A Brief History of Change, 1970–2000*. Penguin Books.

Frankel, J. (2003), *A Proposed Monetary Regime for Small Commodity-Exporters: Peg the Export Price (PEP)*. Harvard University.

Geary, F. (1989), "The Belfast cotton industry revisited." *Irish Historical Studies,* pp. 250–67.

Gill, C. (1925), *The Rise of the Irish Linen Industry.* Oxford: Clarendon.

Grebler, L. (1960), "The housing expansion of 1953–1954: A classic response to easy credit." UMU.

Hamilton, J. D. (1987), "Monetary Factors in the Great Depression." *Journal of Monetary Economics,* pp. 145–69.

Harper, L. A. (1939), *The English Navigation Laws: A Seventeenth-Century Experiment in Social Engineering.* New York: Octagon Brooks.

Hastorf, H., D. Schneider, and J. Polefka (1970), *Person Perception.* Reading, MA: Addison-Wesley.

Hogan, M. (1987), *The Marshall Plan.* Cambridge: Cambridge University Press.

Honnon, K. (2004), "Your local T.D. will never seem quite the same again," in *The Naked Politician,* pp. 4–167. Dublin: Gill & Macmillan.

Honohan, I. (2008), *Republicanism in Ireland: Confronting theories and traditions.* Manchester University Press, pp. 2–103.

Honohan, P. (1999), "Fiscal adjustment and disinflation in Ireland: Setting the macro basis of economic recovery and expansion," in F. Barry (ed.), *Understanding Ireland's Economic Growth.* New York: St. Martin's Press.

Hunter, R. J. (1971), "Towns in the Ulster plantation." *Studia Hibernica,* pp. 49–79.

Irish Railway Commissions (1837), "Second Report of the Commissioners Appointed to Consider and Recommend a General System of Railways for Ireland" (original volume in the National Library of Ireland).

Jacobsen, J. (1994), *Chasing Progress in the Irish Republic.* Cambridge University Press.

Jacobson, D. (1977), "The political economy of industrial location: The Ford Motor Company at Cork, 1912–1926." *Irish Economic and Social History*, pp. 36–55.

Kamery, R. H. (2004), *A Brief Review of the Recession of 1990–1991.* Orlando, FL: Nova Southeastern University.

Kearney, H. F. (1959), "The political background to English mercantilism, 1695–1700." *Economic Review*, pp. 484–96.

Kelly, J. (2003), "The Irish Pound: From Origins to EMU." *Quarterly Bulletin*, Spring.

Kelly, P. (1980), "The Irish Woollen Export Prohibition Act of 1699." *Irish Economic and Social History*, pp. 22–44.

Keynes, J. M. (1933), "National self-sufficiency." *Studies,* pp. 177–99.

Kiefer, D. "Tax cuts and rebates for economic stimulus: The historical record." CRS Report 92-90E.

Kieran, A. (1974), "The Irish economy: The challenges and options." *The Economic & Social Research Institute.*

Kieran, A., T. Giblin, and D. McHugh (1988), *The Economic Development of Ireland in the Twentieth Century.* New York: Routledge.

Killeen, M. J. (1979), "The electronics revelation: Its impact on Ireland," address to Royal Institution of Chartered Surveyors, mimeo.

Kirby.P(2002) The Celtic Tiger in Distress: Growth with inequality in Ireland. Pelgrave

Kliesen K. L. (2003), "The 2001 Recession: How Was It Different and What Developments May Have Caused It?" Federal Reserve, Bank of St Louis.

Kuttner, R. (1999), *Everything for Sale: The Virtues and Limits of Markets.* Chicago: The University of Chicago Press.

Labonte, M., and G. Makinen (2002), "The current economic recession: How long, how deep, and how different from the past?" CRS Report for Congress, Code RL31237.

Lane, P. (2000), "Disinflation switching nominal anchors and twin crisis: The Irish experience." *Journal of Policy Reform,* pp. 301–26.

Lee, J. (1973), *The Modernisation of Irish Society, 1848–1918.* Gill & Macmillan.

Lee, J. (1989), *Ireland 1912–1985: Politics and Society.* Cambridge.

Lucy, K. (1996), "Ireland's software industry poised for next leap." *Irish Times*, December 9.

McArdle P. (2005), "A private sector perspective on the Celtic Tiger." *Group Economics.* Ulster Bank.

McCormick, T. (1989), *America's Half Century: United States Foreign Policy in the Cold War*. Baltimore: Johns Hopkins University Press.

McGibney, A., and F. Ruane (1991), "The Performance of Overseas Industry, 1973–1983," in Anthony Foley and Dermot McAleese (eds.), *Overseas Industry in Ireland*. Dublin: Gill and MacMillan.

McGilligan, P. (1948), Minister of Finance McGilligan's notes on lecture by Paul Bureau, assistant city editor, *News Chronicle*, Irish Institute of Bankers, Dublin, October 1948, p. 35/11.

Minter, W., and L. Shoup (1977), *Imperial Brain Trust*. New York: Monthly Review Press.

Meenan, J. F. (1970), *The Irish Economy since 1922*. Liverpool University Press.

Mjoset, L. (1992), *The Irish Economy in a Comparative Institutional Perspective*. Dublin: National Economic and Social Council.

Monaghan, J. J. (1942), "The rise and fall of the Belfast cotton industry." *Irish Historical Studies*, pp. 1–17.

Murphy, A. E. (2000), "The 'Celtic Tiger' analysis of Ireland's economic growth performance." EUI Working Papers, RSC no. 2000/16.

Murray, A. E. (1903), *Commercial and Financial Relations Between England and Ireland from the Period of the Restoration*. London: PS King and Son.

Ó'Connell, P. (2000), "The Role of the State in Growth and Welfare" in B. Nolan, P. Ó'Connell, and C. Whelan (eds.), *Bust to Boom? The Irish Experience of Growth and Inequality*, Dublin: Institute of Public Administration, pp. 310–39.

O'Donovan, J. (1940), *The Economic History of Live Stock in Ireland.* Cork: Cork University Press.

OECD (1999), Economic Surveys: Ireland.

O'Grada, C. (1997), *A Rocky Road: The Irish Economy Since the 1920s.* Manchester: Manchester University Press.

O'Hagan, J., and C. Newman (2008), *The Economy of Ireland: National and Sectoral Policy Issue, Tenth Edition.* Dublin: Gill & Macmillan.

O'Hagan, J. W., and G. J. Foley (1982), *The Confederation of Irish Industry: The First Fifty Years, 1932–82.* Dublin: Confederation of Irish Industry.

O'Hearn, D. (2001), *The Atlantic Economy: Britain, the US and Ireland.* Manchester: Manchester University Press.

O'Malley, E. (1989), *Industry and Economic Development: Challenge for the Latecomer.* Dublin: Gill & Macmillan.

O'Malley, E. (1992), "Industrial structure and economies of scale in the context of 1992," in J. Bradley et al., *The Role of the Structural Funds: Analysis of Consequences for Ireland in the Context of 1922.* ESRI paper no. 13. Dublin.

O'Malley, E. (1998), "The revival of Irish indigenous industry, 1987–1997." *Quarterly Economic Commentary,* April, pp. 35–60.

O'Riain, S. (1997), "The birth of a Celtic Tiger." *Communications of the ACM*, pp. 11–16.

O'Riain, S. (1999), *Development and the Global Information Society*. Berkeley: University of California.

O'Riain, S. (2000), "The flexible development state: Globalisation, information technology, and the 'Celtic tiger.'" *Politics and Society*, pp. 157–96.

Ó'Sullivan, D. (2000), "Systems Innovation—Managing manufacturing systems redesign." *Journal Computer Integrated Manufacturing*, 13(5): 410–25.

O'Toole, F. (2010), *Enough is Enough: How to Build a New Republic*. London: Faber and Faber Ltd.

Reinhart, C. M., and K. S. Rogoff (2009), "The aftermath of financial crisis." NBR Working paper 14656.

Rothery, B. (1977), *Men of Enterprise*. Dublin: Institute for Industrial Research and Standards.

Ruane, F. (1999), "Whither Ireland's industrial policy?" Paper presented to a conference of the European Network on Industrial Policy. Dublin.

Sherlock, S. (2008), "Dáil committees should have greater role in overseeing Quangos." Press statement. Dublin: Labour Party Press Office, September 15.

66 Business Conference (1967), "Business Representation in Irish National Affairs: The Report of a Study for the 66 Business Conference." Dublin: Harbridge House Europe.

Smith, J. (2010), "'Practice deficiencies' revealed in health authority's inquiry." *Irish Times,* March 8, p. 1.

Ta-Win, L., and J. Schimidt (2002), "Economic Conditions During the 2001 Recession (Part I)." Washington Economic Trends, Research Brief no. 15.

Telesis Consultancy Group (1982), *A Review of Industrial Policy, Report no. 64.* Dublin: National Economic and Social Council.

The Economist (1988), "Survey: Republic of Ireland." January 16, pp. 3–26.

The Journal of Irish Industry (1957), "Federation of Irish Manufacturers: Annual General Meeting," *Irish Industry* 25:2 (February), pp. 39–45.

The Journal of Irish Industry (1959), "The Federation of Irish Manufacturers," *Irish Industry* 27:1 (January), pp. 3–4.

Upgren, A. (1940), "A Pan-American trade bloc," in *Studies of American Interests in the War and the Peace.* New York: Council on Foreign Relations.

Velde, F. R. (2009), "The recession of 1937: A cautionary tale." *Economic Perspectives.* Federal Reserve Bank of Chicago.

Walsh, B. (1996), "Stabilisation and adjustment in a small open economy: Ireland 1979–1995." *Oxford Review of Economic Policy.*

Wexler, I. (1983), *The Marshall Plan Revisited: The European Recovery Plan in Economic Perspective.* Westport, CT: Greenwood.

Whitaker, T. K. (1973), "From protection to free trade: The Irish experience." *Administration,* 21(4), pp. 405–23.

Internet Sources

Bordo, D. M., and D. C. Wheelock (2004), "Monetary Policy and Asset Prices: A Look Back at Past US Stock Market Booms." <http://research.stlouisfed.org/publications/review/04/11/BordoWheelock.pdf> accessed 4 September 2011.

Bordo, M. D., and J. G. Haubrich (2011), "Deep Recessions, Fast Recoveries, and Financial Crises: Evidence from the American Record." <http://www.snb.ch/n/mmr/reference/sem_2011_09_23_haubrich/source>.

Crooks, E. (2010), "US Businesses Urge Irish to Keep Low Tax." <http://www.ft.com/intl/cms/s/0/df703e18-f8c0-11df-b550-00144feab49a.html#axzz1j90ORqI1> accessed 11 December 2011.

Finfacts (2011), "Ireland Top Location for US Multinational Profits." <http://www.finfacts.ie/irelandeconomy/usmultinationalprofitsireland.htm> accessed 12 December 2011.

Hennesy, N. (2011), "Firms Urged to target US deals." *Irish Examiner* (March 17, 2011). <http://www.irishexaminer.com/business/kfeyideysnmh/ rss2/> accessed 11 December 2011.

Honohan, P. "Currency Board or Central Bank? Lesson from the Irish Pound's Link with Sterling, 1928–79." Economic and Social Research Institute. <http://homepage.eircom.net/~phonohan/BNL.pdf> accessed 9 October 2011.

Honohan, P. (2009), "What Went Wrong in Ireland?" Dublin: Trinity College. <http://homepage.eircom.net/~phonohan/What%20went%20wrong.pdf> accessed 9 October 2011.

IDA Ireland (2011), "Ireland and the US Pharmaceutical Industry." <http://www.idaireland.com/news-media/featured-news/ireland-and-the-us-pharma/> accessed 12 December 2011.

IDA Ireland (2011), Ireland and US Investment." <http://www.merrionstreet.ie/wp-content/uploads/2011/05/IDA-Ireland-and-US-Investment.pdf> accessed 12 December 2011.

IDA Ireland (2011) 'Ireland &US Investment': CITI. <http://www.merrionstreet.ie/wp—content/uploads/2011/05/IDA-Ireland-and-US-Investment.pdf> accessed 11 December 2011

O'Leary, Barry (2011). "Ireland and the US pharmaceutical Industry." <http://www.ngpharma.com/article/Ireland-and-the-US-pharmaceutical-industry/> accessed 12 December 2011.

Appendix

This appendix shows that a country's current account balance can be used by policymakers to verify their economic productivity in world economies. The author found that despite the belief that the Celtic Tiger ended because of the 2008 international economic crisis, Ireland's current account balance indicates that the Celtic Tiger ended in 1999.

ECONOMIC PRODUCTIVITY IN THE WORLD ECONOMY

In general, countries record their transactions with other countries using balance of payments. The transactions are recorded as either a credit or a debit. Thus if payments are coming into the country's domestic economy, they are recorded as credits. The records include payments from exports and foreign spending in the domestic economy as well as payments from foreign investments in the hosting country. If payments are flowing out of the domestic economy, it is recorded as a debit. The records include payments on imports, foreign aid, domestic spending abroad, and country investment abroad.

Within the balance of payments, there are three separate categories under which different transactions are recorded. Those categories are the current account, where goods, services, income, and current transfer payments are listed; the capital account, where physical assets such as buildings are recorded; and the financial account, where assets to foreign business are detailed.

By investigating the records of capital and financial accounts of a given country, one can know how markets of that country are regulated, while examining the current account balance (CAB) can indicate to policymakers if a given country's economy is productive. So policymakers can use their country's current account balance to find out the extent of their country's capital market, services, enterprises, or industries and the money coming in from donation or assistance. But at this point, donation or assistance must not be considered as good investments to stimulate economic growth. This is because a sudden failure or an unexpected suspension of donation or assistance (often due to political tensions) will result in cessation of those donations.

The current account balance not only indicates if a country's economy is productive in the world economy, it also shows if a country has a deficit in trade or a surplus. The following equation allows us to know whether the CAB is in deficit or surplus:

CAB = X-M + NYA + NTPA

X = Exports of goods and services

M = Imports of goods and services

NYA = Net income abroad

NTPA = Net transfer payments abroad

A current account balance surplus (CAB = 0) indicates that the country is a creditor to the other countries. This means that a country has abundant resources or its economy is productive, and it is supplying its goods and services to other countries. When a country's current account balance shows a surplus (CAB > 1), this means that country is more productive.

A current account balance deficit (CAB < 0) is an indication that a country is a debtor to other countries. Instead of saving, the debtor countries invest more in other countries in order to meet their investment requirements and domestic consumption. At this stage, however, although the debtor countries are considered to have an unproductive or less productive economy in the global economy, like the United States, some debtor countries are productive in the world economy. This is because their current account balance can result in a deficit as an outcome of their increased capital investments allocated in other countries. For example, when a country sends money to other countries in its investment development, the money sent would be recorded as a debit in the current account, but the future returns from investments made would be recorded as a credit, thus investment income. In other words, a balance deficit could mean that the country is investing more in foreign countries in order to increase its productivity. The United States is more productive in the global economy because of its high level of investments abroad. For example, 90 percent of Irish exports come from American investments based in Ireland.

Table 1 shows that the US trade deficit was significantly reduced during the years of 1982, 1983, 1984, 1989, 1990, 1992, and 1993. In these years, American exports were at a high level, thus the credits recorded in the United States were on the increase. So despite the trade deficit recorded in these years, the American economy was more productive in the world economy.

Table 1 also indicates that the US trade deficit significantly increased in the 2000s. This is an indication that, in addition to the failure of the dot.com bubble, the private business sectors did not recover because the American exports were in decline.

TABLE 1

US CURRENT ACCOUNT BALANCE FROM 1980 TO 2009

Period	Transactions US Dollars (Billions)	Period	Transactions US Dollars (Billions)
1980	2.316	1995	-113.571
1981	5.031	1996	-124.773
1982	-5.533	1997	-140.720
1983	-38.695	1998	-215.066
1984	-94.342	1999	-301.653
1985	-118.159	2000	-416.342
1986	-147.176	2001	-396.596
1987	-160.661	2002	-457.245
1988	-121.159	2003	-519.097
1989	-99.485	2004	-628.521
1990	-78.965	2005	-745.773
1991	2.895	2006	-800.612
1992	-51.614	2007	-710.301
1993	-84.816	2008	-677.134
1994	-121.612	2009	-376.551

Source: IMF, World Economic Outlook Database, 2012

Table 2 indicates that since the 2000s, the Irish economy has been in decline in the global economy. Thus, Irish economic activity was not productive. The fall of Irish economic activity was caused by the 2001 recession, which stemmed from the failure of American industrial production of electronics and software, which in turn triggered a decrease in Irish exports. So although many may think that the Irish economic boom, the so-called Celtic Tiger, was busted in 2008 because of international economic crises, Ireland's current account balance indicates that it lasted for only eight years, from 1992 until 1999.

TABLE 2

IRELAND'S CURRENT ACCOUNT BALANCE FROM 1980 TO 2009

Period	Transactions US Dollars (Billions)	Period	Transactions US Dollars (Billions)
1980	-2.250	1995	2.148
1981	-2.719	1996	2.584
1982	-2.034	1997	2.696
1983	-1.320	1998	0.704
1984	-1.114	1999	0.241
1985	-0.858	2000	-0.350
1986	-0.854	2001	-0.678
1987	-0.035	2002	-1.223
1988	0.019	2003	-0.002
1989	-0.547	2004	-1.078
1990	-0.675	2005	-7.088
1991	-0.025	2006	-7.916
1992	0.392	2007	-13.878
1993	2.005	2008	-14.966
1994	1.763	2009	-6.542

Source: IMF, World Economic Outlook Database, 2012

To Think About

A country's current account balance indicates whether its economic activity is growing or declining in the global economy. Thus, it highlights the country's comparative advantage or benefits in the world economy. If a country's current account balance equals zero, this means that its exports are more than its imports. And this also explains why the country's economy is more productive and has more advantage in the world economy. Thus, the cost of its products are lower than those of other countries. If a country's current account balance is less than zero, that country's imports are more than its exports. The balance less than zero is an indication that a country is not productive in the world economy.

Note

Like the United States, a current account balance less than zero of some countries indicates that they are hosting investments in foreign countries. This means that when policymakers investigate their country's current account balance, it is necessary to examine what caused an increase in their country's credits or debits. At this point, policymakers should know if a current account balance surplus resulted from assistance or foreign aid as well as capital borrowed from foreign capital markets;

it is a warning that the country's economic productivity is in decline in the world economy. Moreover, in order to mitigate an incoming recession, policymakers need to revisit and change if necessary their country's economic strategy every five years.